ON LOCATION....
ON MARTHA'S VINEYARD

ON LOCATION....
ON MARTHA'S VINEYARD

(The Making of the Movie *Jaws*)
50th Anniversary Edition

Edith Blake

BearManor Media
2025

ON LOCATION....
ON MARTHA'S VINEYARD

Copyright © 1975, 2020, 2025 by Edith Blake

"45 Year Later" Copyright © 2020 by Michael A. Smith

Expanded 50th Anniversary Material
Copyright © 2025 by Michael A. Smith

Edited by Michael A. Smith

All rights reserved.

No portion of this publication may be reproduced, stored, and/or copied electronically (except for academic use as a source), nor transmitted in any form or by any means without the prior written permission of the publisher and/or author.

Published in the United States of America by:

BearManor Media

1317 Edgewater Dr. #110
Orlando, FL 32804

bearmanormedia.com

Printed in the United States.

Typesetting and layout by PKJ Passion Global
Cover design by Phil Heeks

ISBN–979-8-88771-759-3

FOREWORD

Here it is, firsthand, the account of how the motion picture *Jaws* was made, and for anyone who sees the motion picture this may well be as indispensable as a libretto at the Metropolitan Opera. Not that *Jaws* on the screen fails to speak adequately for itself, but the making of the film involved quite a different sequence of circumstances and pervasive tone. In a word, as Edith Blake points out, it was a riot. A troubled, surprising, eventful, and hilarious riot.

Mrs. Blake not only saw the action on the Island of Martha's Vineyard where in many long months (not in the originally projected few weeks) the filming was accomplished, at the cost of many odd confrontations and adventures, but she was part of the action. Who fell over backwards into a tub of blood and guts? Cinematrographic blood and guts, of course, but about as inconvenient as the real thing.

This, however, is the least item of her narrative of the spring and summer of *Jaws*. A memorable, definitive, suspenseful, immensely varied and funny exploit of Universal and of all moviedom. Was there ever anything like it? The jury is still out, but no reader of Edith Blake's narrative will doubt the verdict.

Henry Beetle Hough

Edgartown, June 1, 1975

Dedicated

to

Henry Beetle Hough

and the Shark

45^h Anniversary Edition/Expanded 50th Anniversary Edition

Dedicated to

Edith Blake

CONTENTS

Introduction	1
Universal Moves In	5
Script and Filming Start Off in a Dead Heat	15
Angry Armada	23
Tiger Shark	35
East Chop to Menemsha	43
Amity? Town Hall	53
Sea Saga	59
Shark! Shark!	67
On the Beach	73
Fourth of July Beach	79
The Season's On!	84
Back to Bagdad	91
Sea City	100
Sinking Orca and a Stolen Shark	106

All at Sea and a Strike	113
Out In a Blaze of Gory	120
45 Years Later	127
EXPANDED 50TH ANNIVERSARY EDITION	165
Hello, Again	166
Edie	168
One More Look	171

INTRODUCTION

Hello, and welcome to the 45th Anniversary Edition of Edith Blake's best-selling book "On Location....On Martha's Vineyard (The Making of the Movie *Jaws*).

I first "met" Edith Blake in September 1976. I was 16-years old. Barred by my father from making long distance phone calls from home, thanks to a $300-plus bill I racked up talking with a fellow Roy Scheider fan in Kansas City, I walked to the nearby 7-Eleven armed with a roll of quarters and dialed long distance information. I asked for the listing of Edith Blake in Edgartown, Massachusetts and was given the number. After depositing $3.25 "for the first three minutes" – this may sound shocking to those of you reading this that have only known unlimited usage on your cell phones – I waited eagerly as the phone rang. I was greeted with a pleasant "hello" and quickly blurted out who I was and why I was calling. At the time I was helping to run Richard Dreyfuss' official fan club, and I told her that I loved the many "behind the scenes" photos of Richard she had featured in her book. We chatted for a few more minutes – I had to deposit another $1.25 – and then said our goodbyes. Before we hung up, she asked for my address, which I gave her. Needless to say, I was shocked a week later when I came home from school to find a large envelope on my bed. Inside were three photos Ms. Blake had taken during the shoot that weren't included in the book. I still cherish her gift today.

I finally got to officially meet Edie in June 2005 at the first JAWSFest, held on Martha's Vineyard. I had the good fortune of being introduced to her and was able to spend a few moments alone with her. I told her who I was and mentioned the above story and, to my glee, she remembered me. Being a former Boy Scout, I came prepared and produced my copy of her book, which she graciously signed Over the past 15 years I have had the chance to speak with her on several other occasions and every meeting creates a new memory.

Along with Carl Gottlieb's "The *Jaws* Log," Edie's book was one of the first in-depth looks into the making of a feature film. It helped inspire popular "making of" books covering films like *Superman the Movie* (1978), *The Empire Strikes Back* (1980), *Brazil* (1985), *Dick Tracy* (1990) and *Titanic* (1997). It also was a major influence in two other books that feature some of her photographs – "*Jaws*: Memories from Martha's Vineyard" by Matt Taylor and Jim Beller and my own "*Jaws 2*: The Making of the Hollywood Sequel," which I authored with Lou Pisano.

45-years after its premiere on June 20, 1975, *Jaws* continues to gain fans with each successive generation. It is one of those timeless films that pretty much everyone has seen at least once and its impact on pop culture is still being felt today. It has not only spawned a countless number of fans but a countless number of friends as well. If you're reading this book for the first time, I say "welcome aboard!" If you've decided to revisit the adventures within, I say "welcome back!" Amity, as you know, means friendship.

This project would never have come to fruition without the support and friendship of others. Thank you to Edith Blake, for allowing me the honor of sharing her work with new generations; Donna Honig, *Jaws*-doms most favorite Islander and Bow Van Riper of the Martha's Vineyard Museum for sharing many of the new photos featured in this book. Special thanks to Phil Heeks, who not only designed the brilliant cover of this book but was able to clean up 45-year-old negatives to give you, the reader, the best photos possible as well as Chad Godfrey and his staff at Summit Video in Lee's

Summit, Missouri for getting the photos ready for printing. And a special "thank you" to my wife, Juanita, who always manages to tolerate my *Jaws* fixation with a smile on her face.

Michael A. Smith
March 2020

UNIVERSAL MOVES IN

Long before Peter Benchley's 'Jaws" had become a best seller, Brown and Zanuck with Universal Studios had planned to produce the movie version, and art director Joe Alves was stalking the East Coast looking for a town resembling Amity Island in the book.

His research had led him to the hundred square mile Island of Martha's Vineyard, a little backward, surrounded by Nantucket and Vineyard Sounds and beat upon by the restless Atlantic.

Lying just underneath Cape Cod, which stretched a beckoning finger out into the ocean, Martha's Vineyard has lived by whaling, by farming, by fishing, as a port for coastal trade and, of late, as a summer resort.

The Colonial houses, Greek Revival farmhouses and the gingerbread cottages spell out the Island's past when periods of building were interspersed with depressions, thus preventing modernization, just as the Island's inaccessibility prevented progress from raising its ugly towers and fuel tanks.

Therefore, Edgartown, the shire town, remained the perfect New England village of which Peter Benchley had written.

Islanders were just as unaware of Joe Alves' sleuthing as they were of *Jaws*, but when he went back to California in the fall of 1973 he was sketching scenes, frame by frame, with Island sites as background.

When winter descends on Martha's Vineyard it is a time of nothingness. The fall fishing season is over, boats are hauled and those who can afford something better (along with the birds) are apt to be in Florida. Lynn Murphy could not do much to earn a living; he owned a garage, but there was no one about the fishing village of Menemsha who needed a mechanic – things were tough.

Robert Carroll in Edgartown had finally finished building a slabb or gorgeous addition to an old inn, the Kelley House. The addition had gone slowly, managed to run $300,000 over the estimate and not made its planned summer opening until Thanksgiving, so it had been a case of all outgo and no income. The restaurant was an unexpected success, but rooms were vacant – things were tough.

Woodrow Wilson Sayre (grandson of President Woodrow Wilson) is a recent bridegroom now living all year on the Island. Granted, he takes lots of off-Island trips, but they aren't as exciting as when he was assaulting Mt. Everest. He was filling his time by painting his house and acting in amateur theatricals – things were dull.

Barbara Nevin, wife of an Edgartown doctor, found things pretty dull, too. The weather was pretty cold for tennis, her seven children were now on their own. She filled in with various jobs as secretary for a planning group, a restaurant and author Garson Kanin but it was time for something different.

The white stillness of winter hung on – the Island doesn't get much snow but there's a persistence of gray diffused light which is winter.

A few people were watching NBC's "Today" program in February when Peter Benchley was interviewed, and they learned he had written a book about a shark harassing a New England summer resort. This sounded vaguely pertinent. They knew about his father, Nathaniel Benchley, who lived on neighboring Nantucket and who had written a hilarious book called "The Off-Islanders," but there wasn't much interest. The two Islands aren't compatible.

When a month later word was out that the movie would be made on Martha's Vineyard most Islanders didn't have the slightest idea what this would mean. The news came late to hibernating Islanders but Robert Carroll, the president, and Daniel Hall, the executive director, of the Chamber of Commerce were onto something - *Jaws* in its embryo stage had arrived.

Art director Joe Alves, with second director Tom Joyner and the assistant production manager Louis J. "Jim" Fargo, were canvassing the Island, looking for shooting sites previously recommended by Joe. They inspected the fishing village of Menemsha and met the officials, they looked at Cow Bay, and Harthaven and at the same time were tracking down people who would be able to help them, those who could build boats, paint signs, those who knew the politicians, and those interested in theater. They never made notes, never forgot her name, or a face, or what a person did.

One day Joe descended on the Red Cat bookstore to ask if they had any books on cabin cruisers, and Maria Hart said, "No, people around here don't have much interest in stink pots." He then asked if she knew of a Sam Hart who he had heard was the man to contact for permission to use Harthaven. Maria, laughing, had the fun of replying, "He's my husband."

As Alves and Joyner talked to Islanders they were amazed at how open and friendly they were, such great people until they talked to the next guy, who inevitably said terrible things about the first one, and the third one they talked to said terrible things about both the first and the second, and so it went. Eventually they learned not to listen and to take each man for himself.

Brown and Zanuck, the producers, were a successful team. David Brown was the man with an eye for a script and Richard Zanuck was the man to put it all together. Universal Studios was the machinery. William Gilmore was a production manager and, as such, Universal's on-the-spot representative.

Steven Spielberg had been chosen as the director. He and Joe Alves began watching sea movies as soon as they heard they would be doing *Jaws*. Both came to the same conclusion that viewers had come to years ago - the sea scenes looked fake.

Determined to avoid bathtub scenery, they studied special-effects, went to schools and viewed "the ultimate," but even that looked fake. There seemed to be but one solution to the forged look, and that was to do it for real.

The small private harbor at Harthaven looks ideal, sheltered, with little change of tide, away from the maddening throng and prying eyes. It was perfect for capering sharks, nude maidens and sinking boats. No studio tanks for this crew, there were going to do it the hard way. How hard they didn't know.

Letters requesting permission were sent out by Stan Hart (a member of the clan) but the owners wouldn't play. They were not as convinced as the studio that shooting would be finished by the end of June and their harbor would be returned in time for their own summer enjoyment.

Public beaches would therefore have to be used, and one can't keep the public off its own beaches. Various sites would be filmed in the six Island towns so that many permissions must be obtained and the sailing was not always smooth.

As emissaries radiated all over the island, alerting a few Islanders, some in true New England tradition were instantly antagonistic to anything so non-island, but others began getting ideas of joining the invaders.

The doctor's wife, Barbara Nevin, was one of the first to realize that she could be of help since her local knowledge would make her a valuable executive secretary; certainly the job would be different.

For a long time Production wouldn't commit itself, but finally it moved into the empty Kelley House. Bob Carroll had taken Bill Gilmore on a tour of what he had and hit the jackpot. He rented his new house as the production office, the boat shed for construction and his boatyard for nautical endeavors.

Wisely, a cocktail party was held at the Kelley House on March 8 (pre-combat) to let the natives know that the invaders were friendly and were loaded with pretty trinkets. Selectmen from the six Island towns were invited, along with police chiefs, politicians, commissioners and newspaper men. Pacification was the order of the day and friendly fare was served up both to tummies and egos.

A few days later Barbara Nevin lucked her way into an interview with the assistant production manager, Jim Fargo. Yes, she could take shorthand (she didn't tell him she wasn't too good at it). Yes, she knew who was who on the Island (she didn't admit as a doctor's wife she knew more than most). Yes, she was used to a certain mad confusion (after seven children who wouldn't be?).

"It's going to be hard work if I get it," she told her friends. "The long hours won't bother me, because this is finite. Only two months and I'll be back playing tennis by the end of June."

As permission was granted to use public beaches, ponds, boats, docks; to redecorate an Oak Bluffs house, to build a new dock, revamp Edgartown's Main Street (just temporarily), construct a billboard at Gay Head and a full-sized house at Menemsha, production began to tangle with town officials, zoning laws and electric codes so that backs began coming up and a few claws were showing.

As great quantities of lumber, table saws, office equipment, tools, paint, desks, electric typewriters, boats, and dungarees were ordered, the Islanders began to wake up. It was becoming more and more apparent that *Jaws* was not going to be like a few other tame movies and television stuff done on the Island: this was different, this was big, and this had a budget of more than three million dollars, much of which would be spent where Islanders could get it ($30,000 a day just on the Island). Suddenly there were fewer turned up noses, and more turned up palms.

Boys and girls together became instant carpenters and painters, as boats were trundled from their sheltered winter storage at Robert Carroll's boat shed out to the edge of town. Into their space went machines and lumber to build the sets. There were to be a few irate boat owners and a few threatened lawsuits, but the venture saved the boat yard which was financially in a hole.

Then there were irate abutters who complained as lifeguard stands, cabanas, an assortment of hotdog stands, penny arcades and folding houses appeared in the yard. They shed on Fuller Street, in a strictly residential district, was permitted nonconforming use under the zoning code, but making movie sets was too nonconforming. So just as suddenly Jim Fargo, now in permanent residence at the Kelley House, began finding himself in court.

While he struggled and paid fines, Barbara Nevin got her job as secretary and moved along with the office equipment to Bob Carroll's recently purchased house, also in the heart of the residential district, which became the production office. This was proclaimed by a sign with jaws and teeth painted by the Island sign painter, Pete Ortiz, who prefers to make everything Colonial and, Colonial or not, s zoning variance was promptly required for the sign.

There had been rumors about Islanders being needed as actors, so persons with dreams of glory were besieging the Island newspapers and the Chamber of Commerce with questions. When the casting director, Shari Rhodes, arrived at the Kelley House the last weekend in March the word was out, they did NEED ACTORS!!

The Charles J Blairs had recently moved full-time to the island, their new house was finished, painted and they were settled. Like all the others, they were excited when I heard that Jaws would be made on the Island. Theirs was a normal approach, this would be different and fun. Both Chuck and Fanny were just the age to love the movies. In their youth, movies had been good and cheap, and they'd stay glued to double features by the hour, and here was a chance to see themselves on the silver screen.

As soon as they heard that Shari was on hand to do her casting, a few friends started goading Chuck into phoning for an interview. Blue-eyed good-looking Chuck was a yachtsman and perfect, they thought.

Barbara Nevin had a dinner party to which she invited Shari, and Fanny Blairs first move was to invite Shari for dinner. "After all," she said, "what better place to have the casting director that in the bosom of the family."

Dreams of glory got out of hand and long lines formed. When Shari announced there were no glamour girl roles in the movie and men must be clean shaven with shorthair (because otherwise you couldn't tell one from another) a lot of dreams collapsed.

"However," added Shari, "there will be a time when 400 extras are needed."

Shari was an expert at casting and like others in the troupe was fresh from working on *The Sugarland Express* (1974) which was about to win at the Cannes Festival. She firmly believed that no one plays a part better than the real one hence she had cast drunks as drunks, doctors as doctors, photographers as photographers and Selectmen as Selectmen, and that was pretty much the way she did her Island casting.

Pert little Shari from Texas was a redhead with an extra puff on top and looked somewhat like an inverted strawberry. She was instantly the darling of production. The Islanders loved her even when they didn't get the parts they were pining for. She must've had a photographic brain, because she never forgot a name, what a person did or where he lived. Even with a list of 400 names she would be saying, "Yes you're in it - so are you - and you, with your daughter - and you," without ever looking at the list. In the case of families, she already knew who belonged to whom. She was a wonder.

Like the rest of the *Jaws* crew, whether it was night or day, she was never out of blue jeans (some pairs undoubtedly cost more, like those of Steve Spielberg with zippers in all the most outlandish places, which were rumored to have cost $250). Even when setting out by plane for Texas, there was little Shari beaming happily in her blue jeans.

Janice Hull, wife of the executive director of the Chamber of Commerce, and Jini Poole were hired to help her. Janice loved theatrics and Jini was up to her neck in little theater on the Island. Off they went together looking for all the right faces in all the right places, bars at night and waterfronts. One of the first places Shari asked Jini to take her was Menemsha and before she was even out of the car, she spotted Herschel West. Herschel was a bit scruffy and unshaven and perfect for something, Shari didn't know what, but she'd find a place for him. Jini watched expectantly, knowing Herschel and thinking Shari would be rebuffed, but Herschel beamed and then posed for a Polaroid. That night the Larsens had a party and one of them cleaned Herschel up by shaving him, so that when he walked into the production office the next day, everyone exclaimed, "Herschel what have you done?"

At first Shari had an office at the Kelley House, but as that filled with summer people, she was moved to the Harbor View, another hotel operated by Bob Carroll, and eventually moved again, somehow keeping track of all her papers as she moved. Later she appeared daily on the set to see how her choices were working, stacks of papers stashed in a shoulder bag and armed to the teeth with pencils.

When Islanders heard the movie would be made right under their noses their first question was, "Who's in it?"

This went on all summer. "Any big names?" "Anyone we've heard of?"

When Shari was assaulted with this question, she replied that they were in hopes of having Sterling Hayden play Quint, the rough and ragged shark killer. But Sterling Hayden never made it. He was in trouble with the Internal Revenue Service for running off to Tahiti and wasn't to be trusted out of California. So there were no big names for Islanders to brag about.

For *Jaws*, Shari needed the rugged (sometimes ragged) New England types and she was as quick to pick them as she was fascinated by their faces. Craig Kingsbury intrigued her immediately. Craig, like most of the Islanders, was a part-time fisherman and a part-time farmer, doing one when it was impossible to do the other. He had a swaggering personality with the cussed independence of a New Englander and had gained a certain Island notoriety for his importation of skunks that heretofore had not been present.

A few of the yachting types with yachting records a mile-long, like Chuck Blair, didn't hold a candle to the real working Islanders with their crusty New England faces. With little more than a form and a Polaroid print, Shari kept track of hundreds of rustic faces which descended on her for days. Those she especially liked she asked to read before passing them on to Steve Spielberg.

While she interviewed the man, Janice Hull made order out of chaos by herding them to a waiting room supplying them with a form to record their names, phone numbers, and acting experience. While vainly trying to work an ill-tempered Polaroid, she told the plot.

"Four hundred people will stampede... chased by a shark... then destroy each other in panic!"

The scene sounded pretty rough, and how were 400 people going to get into the water at the end of June? It was impossible, what with rehearsals and retakes, the water would still be in the 60s if that.

"No way," thought a Girl Photographer, was she going to miss taking pictures of 400 blue people in ice water with a white shark. But something stirred - there was a foreboding. She must be sure she wasn't one of those 400. (When the day came - she was).

All through April Shari cast and tripped to Boston to hire extras belonging to the Screen Actors Guild, or members of SAG as local extras soon learned to call them.

Members of SAG got paid $45 a day as extras against $20 for non-members. The non-members looked a good deal more the part of Islanders and as Islanders they had no transportation and housing problems.

While casting went on at the Kelley House, up in the woods in a log cabin, Steve and Carl Gottlieb wrote the script. Together they wrote right up to the first day's shooting, and from then on at night or on the set.

Then, just before shooting was begun, the part of Quint, the rugged rugged shark fisherman, was cast, and English actor (the Shakespearean type) Robert Shaw took the part. He had just finished *The Sting* (1973), another film by Brown and Zanuck, which was well on its way to being a huge success.

SCRIPT AND FILMING START OFF IN A DEAD HEAT

It is most unusual in a multimillion-dollar feature movie to go into production with so little preparation - no stars, no script, no shooting schedule. But the unions, often the root of problems, where the reason.

The previous fall there had been a writer's strike which lasted for about five months and when it was over there was no product left to feed to movie and television makers, so in tremendous haste scripts had to be written and stories filmed.

Production was terrified that this would happen again. If the actors went out on strike it might be months, even a year, before they can make *Jaws*, and *Jaws* had to be made while the story was hot. It was too good an idea (sharks were becoming fascinating reading) and Peter Benchley's novel was still high on the best-selling lists.

Also, a movie about swimmers being munched on by sharks was not winter fare; it should be served in the spring and early summer just as people were taking to the water in ordinary course. The whole thing would have more impact if it scared everyone half to death in the process of educating them about what was in the water along with them.

Therefore, Production went into production in a half prepared state, begging for confusion. Steve Spielberg and Joe Alves were both 26, so they could take the strain of working night and day, always just one step ahead of what was going to be shot the following day.

The fact that Steve is an opportunist didn't lessen the confusion. While directing he's quick to see a scene's potential as a springboard for something else. His latest success, *The Sugarland Express*, had all the flavor of the Keystone Cops fringed with slapstick and packed with situations that must've arisen while filming, although Steve swears it's all true and the script was only changed twice from real life.

One thing the crews did know before shooting started was everything there was to know about sharks, and each truck seemed to have its own shark library, to the point where the Teamsters could tell a blue from a basking, and which bit and which didn't.

The Teamsters composed an entire division, seemingly on their own, called transportation, and they transported all the other unions, including the actors and producers, which tended to give many Islanders the impression that these Hollywood people were a bunch of rich slobs with chauffeurs.

The movie business is full of unions. Everyone in it is a member of the International Alliance of Theatrical and Stage Employees which is divided into two groups, the East Coast and the West Coast, and never the two shall interchange without a hullabaloo. IATSE, as it is called, is composed of carpenters, electricians (gaffers), stagehands (grips). costumers, makeup men, art departments, wardrobe, special-effects, cameramen, directors and actors, each in their own union., compounded by the ever-present Teamsters.

Since Bill Butler, the director of photography (DP) was from California, the East Coast union had to send a DP also, who is paid thousands just to stand by and do nothing while each man who operated a camera was duplicated by the East and West unions.

Each union is snippy about its job, and actually doesn't like a helping hand from an outsider, even when it's offered with the best intentions. Islanders quickly learned that it was wisest not to do anything they weren't paid to do.

Although each man was a member of the union, he was also his own boss and as a freelancer signed a contract for the films he chose. This meant that many of them had never worked together and when they met off set the remark was always, "what you do?"

The most fascinating union rule was the one which required that a hot sit-down lunch be served every day. No matter where they worked; on the beach, in a house, out in the rain or at sea, there was that hot sit-down lunch, and was it good!

With casting keeping one jump ahead of filming, Jonathan D. Filley didn't know he even had a part, or that he would be in the opening scene Thursday morning until Tuesday evening.

For years Jonathan's parents and grandparents had been summer-comers to the satellite island of Chappaquiddick, which forms the other side of Edgartown harbor. Jonathan had gone to the Brook School, where he did a lot of theatricals, and after graduation he was studying at Boston University only a two-hour drive and two ferry rides from Chappaquiddick. Through his brother Patrick, who works at Doubleday, Jonathan learned that the movie would be made on Martha's Vineyard and extras would be needed. Therefore, he was available and contrived to be out on the Island when Shari Rhodes arrived to start casting.

Jonathan is tall, good-looking, with shoulder length blonde hair, the clean-cut product of a private school and perfect for the part of the rich young prep schoolboy from Tuxedo Park off with friends on a summer holiday.

After Shari had heard him read she passed them on to the producers, Brown and Zanuck, from whom he had departed with the distinct feeling "don't call us we'll call you."

Weeks had passed and hope had fled when, as he was painting the leather store across the street, he got word that Shari was looking for him. He bolted.

"Man, you got here quickly," she said as she handed him his script. This was on Tuesday afternoon and shooting was to start Thursday morning at the crack of dawn and he was to be in the first scene playing Cassidy, the rich boy whose girl gets sharked.

Wednesday night Jonathan was a nervous wreck with no way to work it off because he given up smoking six weeks before. The ferry from Chappy over to Edgartown doesn't start running until 7 a.m., so he had to drive a truck along the sands of South Beach (which now connects the two islands) to Katama and then into Edgartown where the Teamsters were to pick him up the Kelley House and drive him right back to Katama. Union rules say that a bit player must arrive courtesy of Transportation, not truck. The Teamsters sometimes have an ego problem.

Jonathan made it to the Kelley House by 6 a.m. but his nerves were still in a state when he walked in and spotted the cigarette machine. That was his first mistake. Then he saw Freddy Zendar and thought, "Gee, these Hollywood guys sure are kooks. I hope this one doesn't make a pass at me." That was his second.

Freddy Zendar, small with longish blonde-white hair, brown leather skin (from many years on the water) and at that moment suffering from an overdose of sun, did look strange, particularly at 6 a.m. when anything looks odd if you're not used to the hour. Freddy was a technical consultant on things maritime and turned out to be the "greatest."

When he arrived at Katamat, for the second time that morning, Jonathan found that he had been assigned a dressing room with his name over the door. That helped the nerves; they really were expecting him.

When he chatted with Steve Spielberg and Roy Scheider, who was to play the scene with him, his nerves completely disappeared so he started having fun.

Roy Scheider was playing the police chief, Martin Brody, and the two were to amble down the deserted beach (a crew of 100 was there to help them) gathering pieces of clothing dropped by Jonathan's girl, Chrissie, as she headed for her midnight swim.

The 19 miles of South Beach that May 2nd morning in no way resembled its usual summary self. The air was crystal clear and blowing an arctic air mass, while the small parking place at the end of Katama Road looked like lower Fifth Avenue with trucks galore and even a bus. Some of the smaller trucks had been rented, and by skillful administration of masking tape, "Avis" had been converted to "Jaws." The huge trucks belonged Universal Studios and had been driven (by the Teamsters, of course) the 3000 miles from the Pacific to the very angry edge of the Atlantic.

Islanders were not pleased by this. They had just gone through a nasty siege of the fuel shortage, cutting back on electricity, heat and gas and here these giants had been driven across the continent. Any protests were quickly growled aside with, "Well we have to make a living."

When Production had said there would be trucks to park, no one had envisioned the size or the quantity; this was not the mainland. The roads and streets were not going to be big enough! "How did they get these over on the ferry," querried the spectators. Anyway, there they were containing everything that could ever be needed. There was a carpentry shop, dressing rooms, electrical shop, restrooms, medical supplies, lumber, miles of thick electric cables, generators, cameras, dollies, lights and lunch.

A commissary truck with two big stoves and three ice boxes was the galley, towing a small truck containing the dining tables and chairs. It was to feed the multitudes, not in picnic style customary in South Beach but in sit-down dinner-party style as required by the rules, and it continued to feed between 160 and 200 people six days a week for the next 4 ½ months.

About 100 persons were on the se- really a dune - half from California and half from the unions of New York. The men, working always at a leisurely pace, seemed to know what they were doing, although they did not know each other, and all looked like chaos as miles of heavy electric cables were laid through the dunes and a perfectly level wooden track was stretched on the beach for a 200-foot run for the camera dolly. Alongside lumbered the huge arc lights on sand dollies with large tires. As the men slugged down in the sand there often calls of "no violation" as help was needed from other unions.

There were only four women on the set; the nurse, Helen Jackson (Edgartown already had one nurse named Helen Jackson), the script girl, Charlsie Bryant (who is now called a script supervisor because of equal rights: men do it too), the assistant second director Barbara Bass and the Girl Photographer, spying for the Vineyard *Gazette*.

Barbara Bass is the first female director in the union who passed through the union school scrapping all the way. She is a graduate of Smith, where she was coxswain of the crew. Her first job was in New York working as a special investigator for Mayor Lindsay, and this to Barbara met running down all the complaints about garbage collection while the things that really mattered went untouched. She was beginning to get pretty peeved when she lucked into a film crew needing local knowledge, and overnight she was an assistant director. She did independent films for a year before it was suggested she would make about five times as much as a member the union. That was fine, but Barbara knew they had never taken a woman into the two-year training program.

Thinking she had nothing to lose she took the exam and came in number one, ahead of thousands of applicants. Then for six months she didn't work a day until she had proof that she was being discriminated against, whereupon she declared war and with an army of cohorts stormed a board meeting. Now she is a member of the East Coast branch of the union about to transfer to the West Coast.

Barbara hadn't been on the island too long when she was working in the leather goods store one afternoon planning to turn it into a music shop (courtesy of *Jaws*) when Jonathan Filley walked in. Those present said instant sparks flew and they were still flying when the pair left for Hollywood in December.

Probably for the lack of a script the first day shooting was similar to the beginning of the novel and covered the discovery of the remains of Chrissie, the shark's first victim (the remains got toted about most of the day in a blue plastic garbage bag and looked pretty sloppy) to the closing of the beaches by the mayor and selectmen. The mayor was not an Islander, but the selectmen were, and true to

Shari's casting they were past and present selectmen from Edgartown.

It was suggested several times that Bob Carroll play the mayor, but he turned it down feeling that with hotels, restaurants and boat yards he had enough to do. Murray Hamilton, a professional actor, was hired instead and throughout the scenes of political harangue he kept asking Bob "why the hell didn't you play the mayor, your perfect."

The first scene on the beach was rehearsed a few hundred times, not only to drill Roy Scheider and Jonathan Filley, but to rehearse camera and light crews. It wasn't easy; the lights kept getting stuck in the sand and strange bumps kept invading the camera track.

After the rehearsals 20 takes were made of the action until the director got what he wanted and nothing had gone wrong with the radio microphones worn by the actors, so the sound men got what they wanted.

Since the two principals were supposed to be alone on an empty beach the 200 footprints left by the crew and light dollies had to be brushed out by a bunch of broom wielders after each of the 20 takes.

When the footprints had been demolished the assistant director, Tom Joyner, would bellow through his bullhorn, "Quiet! Ready to roll, no wait a minute, Bill give us some seagulls," and Bill behind a dune would throw out bread until the Katama gulls were sated.

The repeating scene played to a constantly changing supply of sidewalk superintendents congregating on the dunes to stand fascinated in the face of the Atlantic gale for hours waiting, watching and trampling the precious beach grass. Their eyes pirouetted from the large arc lights in the blinding sun to the orange and white striped cabanas, the trucks, the hordes of humanity and the turmoil used to take one scene which would be on the screen for seconds.

Adding to the conglomeration of people were those involved in different scenea scheduled for that day. These included the selectmen, who'd been made up, and now lounged near the portable dressing rooms wondering what was happening to their businesses. Things were certainly badly organized, they thought, they were not used to the theater. Later they got pretty blasé about dashing off to "location."

The first scene lasted until lunch which had the Islanders and spectators flabbergasted as the actors all sat down to their hot meal served in the parking lot among the trucks, between the dunes, in the teeth of the icy Atlantic in an area heretofore used solely for picnics.

The wind shifted to onshore, and the light changed. The Islanders had noticed and were concerned, but the movie people hadn't, so there were comments by the sidewalk superintendents. "Don't they see, the water is different, the light is different?" But the movie people didn't see and the shooting went on while it got a hell of a lot colder.

Chrissie's "remains" were discovered by Hendricks, a policeman played by Jeff Kramer, and they included a real arm still attached to Andrea Morton, a waitress from the Kelley House. She had been soaking it in a bucket of water for hours and in the cold it was rapidly turning blue without benefit of makeup.

Shooting was continued through the long light of a May evening until the last glimmer left the lens and then, like the Arabs, the studio picked up its orange and white cabanas, packed itself back into its trucks, and stole the 3 miles back into Edgartown. The beach and dunes were their old selves again, tracked by ruts and footprints, but the scars of combat were quick to vanish in the freshening breeze.

ANGRY ARMADA

The next day found the whole entourage on Bob Carroll/s dock at the Norton and Easterbrooks Boatyard. At this time of year it should have been splashed with new paint, smelling of new cordage, with the hoist running day and night as boats were readied for summer. Instead, it was packed with *Jaws*.

The same congregation of mammoth trucks now lined a narrow street, this time in the heart of the snappiest summer houses (the boat yard is also zone for nonconforming use). The rows of staid white whaling captains mansions, all more than a century old, looked down on a hive of activity which must've seemed slightly reminiscent of all the paraphernalia, provisions, gear, equipment and people necessary to ready the crammed whale ships for eternal voyages.

What Production termed the Armada scenes were to be shot for a week or more, but it had to be off the dock by May 15. That was final.

At this point in the story a reward had been offered for the capture (dead or alive) of the shark which had just consumed a small child of whom its mother was quite fond. Therefore, all manner of the town's rabble, with all equipment, in all matter of craft (none of it seaworthy 0 to the seed to rid it of the great white shark bent on ruining Amity Island's summer economy.

Most of the residents along the harbor front had been asked to lend their docks to accommodate 100 extras and 50 small boats. As it turned out, the boats were so small that they all fitted into the yard's boat basin. When Sheri Rhodes came down and saw them, she looked like a bad puppy and almost whispered, "I thought 50 boats would look like a lot more than that."

The atmosphere was delightful, the hundred extras, the hundred crew members, the loitering Teamsters and a collection of autos made the dock into a carnival. Snaking through all this were laid the inevitable electric cables over which tripped the still photographer, Lewis Goldman, with his Polaroid, recording the placing of everything so that it could be placed there again for continuing scenes and retakes.

Crisscrossing the scene where the coffee drinkers making their way back and forth to the urn and shredding their empty Styrofoam cups into the harbor where they were promptly devoured by the harbor mallards which acted a bit odd for several days thereafter.

Even after having Shari for dinner, Chuck and Fanny Blair didn't get speaking parts but they were recruited for a shark posse. Their call was for 7 but they had heard that several cars would be needed for background at the end of the dock, so they hurried down to get theirs into the act at $10 a day.

Fanny was stationed in a boat with Erford Burt, which spoke well for her safety, and Chuck flung himself in the smallest of sailboats.

"Do you know how to sail it?" pensively asked Jim Fargo, which brought hoots from the natives on the dock. It was a laughing matter; not only was Chuck one of the best, but if that boat was going to keep up with the rest of the fleet she was going to do it with whatever persuasion she could get from her two horsepower outboard and not her sail.

Bouncing Woodrow Wilson Sayer was in the posse and arrived in his Mount Everest climbing boots (which he had worn pretty much since he made his assault). Sporting a large rifle and a small fishnet, he streamed down the dock along with Mrs. William C Bowie (Edgartown's pretty hostess with the moistest); she in thin white pants and a cyclamen slicker, toted a picnic basket chic enough for a picnic with Mr. Pickwick.

John Alley, who should have been tending the store (he owns the grocery in West Tisbury) was scheduled to bellow at people docking boats in the wrong slips. He did it for about two days and thought the whole thing was pretty silly and quit.

Stan Hart got a role even though he hadn't gotten Harthaven as a shooting site, and dressed inappropriately in a sports jacket, courtesy of wardrobe, was acting the perfect host and handing ladies and gear about with neat aplomb. John Painter looked absolutely fierce clad in bullets, and Bill O' Gorman staggered about with strings of dynamite. As this madness ensued, Donald Poole, as harbormaster, sat quietly munched a bowl of cold cereal, looking a bit like a television commercial. He had been coerced into being an extra by his daughter-in-law, Jini Poole.

She often found him chattering away with Steve Spielberg and finally asked, "How come you're so lucky and always get to talk to Steve?" "Who's Steve?" was his inevitable reply.

Jini herself was one of the extras because Shari thought she would enjoy seeing how they did things in the movies as opposed to the theater.

Willis Gifford, who arrived spotless in creased pants and new sneakers, was instantly attacked by the makeup man with dirt in an aerosol can and then handed a fishing rod for minnows. Chuck Blair also had a fishing rod until he lost it and was docked his first days' pay for losing a prop.

In need of eateries, it wasn't long before the crew discovered the Black Dog restaurant in Vineyard Haven and thereby Allan Miller, who was to work with Production pretty much most of the summer. Had he known them better in the beginning he might have said something when he was first handed a double-headed harpoon. It looked odd, but then everything in the scene was madness, so why not double-headed harpoons?

The harpoons reputedly had been ordered from the South St., Seaport in New York, but bringing harpoons to Edgartown is like taking harpoons to Nantucket, New Bedford or Sag Harbor - that's where they came from in the first place, and almost every summer cottage has one as a decoration or a fire poker.

By the time the art directors learned that they had been using phony harpoons, the scenes had been shot (and re-shot) so many times that there was not a chance that anyone would tangle with them again.

With all the people in the movie waiting around for something to happen and all the people who had come to see what was happening, the set began to take on all the aspects of a social event. Islanders who hadn't seen each other throughout the dullness of winter chatted as they watched and waited.

The Fleas, so-called because they once owned a flea market, commented that all the Islanders were playing caricatures of themselves.

The first scene of the hordes eagerly or anxiously charging down to their boats was shot 14 times.

"No wonder they all go nuts out in Hollywood," remarked another spectator. Stan Hart helped some old ladies and their gear into a too small boat. "We'll go again," came the word from the bullhorn and Stan would unload the boat and the ladies just in time to do it all over again and over again and again until he began to lose track of which way he was loading.

To add to the melee, Freddy Zendar was trying to teach Richard Dreyfuss, who played Hooper, the oceanographer from Woods Hole, to bring a speedboat into a dock. Dreyfuss had never seen a boat in the water before (it seemed) and it wasn't working. Both the boat and the dock were fast becoming the worse for wear and Islanders were dryly remarking, "Hollywood people sure can't handle boats."

To save time, property, perhaps life and everyone's sanity it turned out to be easier for Freddy to bring the boat in blind, crouching under the dashboard, while Rick Dreyfuss just looked as if he were in control. Even the old-time salts were impressed by Freddy's no see, eggshell landing.

While the actors were filmed while speaking their lines, the extras were filling in the background with activity known as atmosphere, and supposedly organizing themselves for a shark hunt. Everything had to be rehearsed by the principals, then by the extras and then altogether. Next it had to be filmed and this took shivery hours.

Then after lunch the rains came, and the extras were delighted; they can now go home and get warm. But Production had other ideas and had sneakily bought up all the foul weather gear in town, so the shooting continued. The new scenes had to match their predecessors, so blue filters went over the lights and the yellow oil skins could only be worn between the takes.

Tom Joyner's bullhorn would roar, "ready to roll, get rid of the yellow," causing one participant to sing out, "I wonder where the yellow went?"

After 10 hours they had made 140 seconds of the movie. Working with boats, gear and 100 extras was time-consuming as Universal was about to learn.

The next day at 7 sharp they were all back at it again, consuming pots of coffee to keep warm, and wearing the same thin summer close (for continuity - it was supposed to be the same hot summer day, but it was colder). Stan Hart noted that his inappropriate sports jacket had somehow been dried out and pressed but those not dressed by wardrobe had to manage getting their clothes dry enough to wear the second day. The weather was pretty much the same - unattractive. This was Saturday so the collection of sidewalk superintendents grew to proportions needing bleachers..

More scenes were taken for atmosphere. Fanny Blair sat in her prop, a boat, and during non-takes did a crossword puzzle. Robert Shaw arrived from Ireland to check out playing the part of Quint and viewed the extraordinary set with big eyes and shook his head. Richard Zanuck and David Brown (there was already a David Brown in Edgartown) walked about the set, or the dock, encouraging something to please happen since this was costing $1000 a minute, and Eleanor Harvey spent another day cramped in a boat almost too small to float.

Eleanor is a large woman and a competent boatman. It was not her fault -the boat was just not the right size. In summer, for more years than most can count, she is, of all things, a lady garbage collector, going to all the visiting boats in the harbor in the mornings and opening clams at the Edgartown Yacht Club for the rest of the day. She has therefore become one of those characters known up-and-down the New England seaboard. Since this obviously was in summer, Eleanor had the time to spend wedged in a boat absorbing the rain is a day player. She was pleased with being a day player, which meant she had lines and was getting $138 a day against the pittance of the extras.

Teddy Grossman, the stuntmen, got into the act that day as a drunk. Warmed underneath by a wetsuit, he staggered down the dock swinging an ice bucket and a huge bag of popcorn. To the tune of Steve yelling, "Funnier!" He staggered forward. "Funnier!" He swayed limply. "Funnier!" He boarded a boat, miraculously still on his feet. He pitched forward, oops, then steadied and just when it looked as if he had made it, he tripped backwards over a dock line and sailed overboard in a cloud of popcorn.

Irvin W. Rose (Rosie) of Wardrobe was standing by with a blanket and a dry set of identical clothe for retakes, but the scene was a "print." Everyone cheered; they were learning the jargon and print meant that at least it might get to the cutting room floor.

As people mulled about and did nothing, a dilapidated fishing boat named Scup Bucket (she looked like one) appeared at the dock and camera crews and directors, like delighted boys, jumped aboard. This was the beginning of their sea-saga summer. How little they knew, how long they would struggle, how many hours they would spend salt-soaked, cold, sunburnt, hot, rocked, bounced and battered. That day all was new, things were still going well.

"Into the boats and follow me!" yelled the bullhorn, so into the boats for real went the extras to follow the camera out into the harbor with a loop around the red nun off the lighthouse, then back to do it again and again. The extras bellowed and brandished their weapons; bombs, harpoons, fishing poles, guns and bows and arrows, while the dogs barked. "Islanders," Shari noted, "go everywhere with their dogs, so why not on a shark hunt?"

Saturdays and Sundays are usually days off in Hollywood, but on location only Sunday is a day of rest. This posed a problem to the movie people. Edgartown is a small town, and out of season it is smaller so that not a darn thing is open after 6 p.m. except the liquor store. Since they worked from sun-up to sundown, this left no time to get to the drugstore, the launderette or to buy groceries (Kelly House food costs too much for everyday dining). Then on Sundays, their day off, everything in strict New England fashion was closed.

On the first Saturday night, there is no doubt they howled. Great boxes of liquor and cartons of beer were lugged out of the Harborside Liquor store, a bit eye-opening for the proprietor, who suddenly found himself with a healthy unexpected source of revenue.

Sunday there was nothing to do and no place to go. Those who could handle the pesky things rented bicycles and wobbled through the streets with the rest of early teenage tourists who usually infest the Island spring and fall.

Three men went into the paper store, the only store open (for only two hours) and bought 35 kites. Small-town stuff for the big-town boys, and unexpected revenue for the new owner of the store.

Monday found a little fleet offshore bouncing and bobbing in gray seas so angry that only two takes were made before the Armada returned to the harbor and the camera moved to the stability of *Jaws* headquarters and Bob Carroll's and Greek Revival house where filming was done in the mini police station, concocted on the ground floor of the more than 100-year-old building.

Normally the camera was followed by its retinue of trucks which parked outside the office on the corner of Winter and Summer streets just a block from Main Street and directly across the street from St. Andrews church.

It must be remembered that Edgartown is the unspoiled, classic, pretty New England town. These are the same streets where tourists amble in summer admiring the old white houses set side-by-side on the edge of the street bounded by picket fences, embroidered with roses, and shaded by giant elms.

Main Street is the same, still retaining many of the old white houses, or the Victorian stores with false fronts. There is no wide highway on the island and the speed limit is 45 miles an hour.

The next day the fleet sailed again. The weather really wasn't much better, but the water was less bumpy. The script called for Ben Gardner, the only real fisherman in the posse, to outdistance the cacophonous parade and encounter the shark, whereupon he has a heart attack and is next seen on the bottom.

This part was played by Islander Craig Kingsbury and since one can't act dead on the harbor bottom, a specialist in such things was flown up from New York to make a death mask of Craig, which was duly attached to a make-believe body.

His boat, Flicker, was sunk and then promptly pumped out and hauled back to the dock, well scarred with tooth marks along the gunwale to be preserved in case of retakes. Islanders at the dock who viewed this shoddy craft only found more evidence that the movie people didn't know what they were doing around boats.

Jaws people were not the only ones. The British Broadcasting Company crew arrived that day to do a documentary on the filming of *Jaws* and in the process of leaping from boat to boat, one man missed.

The next day's shooting was really far out (Production was trying to outdistance land) off Cape Pogue, a point of land at the end of nowhere which juts off from Chappaquiddick into the wild seas bounded by rocks, shoals and a roaring current. It is not really the best of places to be in a boat any time, but at this stage of the game Production still thought that this was where most of the sea shooting would be done. It seemed ideal. No land in sight except to the rear of a picturesque lighthouse when needed, no boats on the horizon (it was still too early for those), marvelous color and seas which looked like the real McCoy (because they were).

The plot called for the extras in the little boats to be chumming for shark, but Production hadn't known just when the chum would be needed. They had long ago alerted Everett Poole, Jini's husband, that they would be needing quantities of the stuff and he replied that he didn't always have that much and couldn't get it on instant notice. (Instant notice was the way Universal wanted everything)

So the chum was ordered well in advance of when it would be needed and when it got smelly Production was going to throw it out, but Everett show them how to salt it down. It'd been in such condition on the dock since Friday, and this was Wednesday, so to say the least it was smelly as hell. Then to make things more unattractive it'd been made up with blood by Max Factor from Del Armstrong's ever ready spray can.

The poor extras went through a nasty, smelly, slimy operation out there in the cold, sunless air and bouncy seas and all sorts of vague excuses were dreamed up as to why certain persons were quite unable to handle the chum.

This was not the nicest known way to spend a spring, and the interesting thing is that so many people did. The question, of course, is why; certainly it wasn't for $20 a day. John Alley had said, "this is crazy" and quit, but he was the only one. Dainty and pretty indoor type (Edgartown's hostess with the most this) Mrs. William C. Bowie, stuck it out and it must've been harder on her than any of the others, for this wasn't her dish of tea.

Shooting continued, and so did the cold. Janice Hull was excited because she had been promoted from an extra to a playing part and given a few lines to yell and a few fists to shake. She and Richard Hewitt had a battle over who had hooked the shark first and in reality they had hooked each other.

Cherry bombs were used to sound like rifle shots by those shooting at the shark, they didn't sound as loud out at sea as they did in the studio lot, so something louder had a be found. Already people on the shore were claiming they had seen depth charges, and what were those crazy movie people doing now?

Just about this time, in the waters of Cape Pogue, the problems the land- oriented producers hadn't counted on began to show; WATER, WIND and TIDE.

Stan Hart was at the helm of his own boat which was being used as camera boat number two, along with the larger Scup Bucket as camera boat number one. The crews and scene were all lined up ready to take with the camera boats side-by-side when the tide invaded the best laid plans. Scup Bucket, being the larger, didn't drift at the same pace as Stan's smaller boat, therefore he was out of line. If he backed her down to adjust his boat, the cameramen bellowed because their precious Panaflex cameras would be doused was saltwater; if he proceeded to the loop around to where he should be, they would yell "what the hell you doing? We just missed a great take!" No one cared about explanations.

The waves and tide, shifting seas and boats became a problem which lasted throughout the shooting, which lasted throughout the summer, causing hours of frustration as scene after scene was carefully set up only to be swept askew by a shift of current. The Islanders knew about such things and certainly would not have picked Cape Pogue for the opus, but the boys from California "just don't listen." This was a phrase to be uttered often.

As the boats shifted off Pogue in the cold, a man-made problem slowly came to light. The makeup man, Del Armstrong, had wisely packed his bottles and jars (which should of contained makeup) with something for the cold - brandy. Hence, as hands and feet tend to go numb, the call oft went out for the brandy bottle until it always wasn't just used for the cold.

All this was fine for the first day's freeze, but the following morning when she arrived on the set, Fanny Blair noticed a small plastic glass in the crotch of a tree. "Looks as if someone had a wild night down here," said Chuck. "No," said Fanny, who had spotted an ice cube in the glass and then sniffed it. "Somebody's started early." It seems that Woody Sayre, taking the hint from Del, had arrived with a bottle of Gilbey's gin. "Good God!" said Stan Hart, "you can't drink that stuff straight!" "It's not straight gin," claimed Woody, "it's a martini. I put five drops of vermouth in it." Stan himself wasn't that well prepared, but he had picked up two cans of beer at the Girl Photographer's on the way over. "Just for thirst," he told her.

Each day the little boats and their bedraggled contents came back to the boatyard dock for their hot lunch and the honey wagon. If the weather was too foul for dining alfresco it was often served instead at St. Andrews parish house. The extras walked while the principals were driven by Transportation in buses, station wagons and a yellow and white Jeep with the legend "Amity Island Police" on its doors. (No reason not to get some use out of the props). Production obviously planned to sell it after the movie since the price list remained glued to the window all summer.

As the cold increased it was discovered that the Harborside Liquor Store (in this case the Liquorside Harbor Store) opened at 8 a.m. and was within walking distance of wherever lunch might be served.

There has always been a lot of talk about ancient sailors and their rum and modern sailors and their grog - the two seem to go so well together. The habits of sailors past and present may be myth, but it is true that, preceded by a day of bouncing on the briny, grog becomes a lot more effective.

Whatever the reason (that was the afternoon Brown and Zanuck came out to see what was taking so long) there were a few dangerously scrambled hours out beyond Cape Pogue and fewer extras on the set the rest of the week.

It was several days later that an incident which nearly dampened the spirits - as well as the cameras - was avoided, so in no way can the action be attributed to the foregoing problem. The situation arose when a boat not named the Andrea Doria decided to behave like her.

All the little boats were told to "charge" toward the Oak Bluffs water tower and Henry Carreiro's boat was to speed through the fleet with the camera boat light alongside. As the camera boat closed the gap, trying to get in closer, Henry's boat swerved, nearly swamping a sailboat and, over correcting, hit the camera boat. In the bump the camera and cameramen nearly went overboard. As she recoiled, two little boats trying to keep clear ran into each other and one young man went halfway overboard, his hands down with the propeller, while two boats trying to get away from Henry's boat enacted the domino theory. A man started to go overboard backwards so the helmsman reached for him and in so doing hit the throttle and lost control of the wheel. The craft then (with the bit in its teeth) spun out of control wide open into the rest of the fleet. (More evidence of the domino theory).

When it had all subsided, the boy held up his hands to show the worried watchers he still had all his fingers.

"That's the end of this day's work," agreed the seafaring extras and so they were nonplussed to hear Tom Joyner calmly command, "starting places please."

During the confusion, the Panaflex camera was flung under a chair and, in complete agreement that the show must go on, photographed the webbing underneath.

Maybe because the weather had been so unsettled during the filming of the Armada scenes, the blues and grays of the sea and sky could not be matched, or perhaps for 60,000 other reasons Barbara Nevin received word in February that the Armada scenes might not be used in the movie.

TIGER SHARK

The organized madness which was afloat and ashore continued as the plot unfolded. There was a contagiousness to the mood, and Islanders regularly stopped by to spectate when the filming was on the Norton and Easterbrooks dock, and peered anxiously sea word when it was not.

Jaws attracted the news world, so that reporters Dropping in or overboard with regularity.

Filming turned out to be the longest social "do" the Island had ever seen. People got to know a whole different crowd as they chatted comfortably with strangers, so that the spectators and extras enjoyed themselves to no end.

Jeff Kramer, who played the police chief's assistant, is an Island boy, the grandson of Henry Cronig, an Island entrepreneur in the days before Bob Carroll. Jeff now lives in New York where he is a real actor.

He happened to read about *Jaws* being made on the Island in the Vineyard *Gazette* and promptly stirred his agent into action. Then he junketed to Boston to meet Shari Rhodes and won his part. He was delighted for now he could have more time on the Island. Like all Vineyarders, full or part-time, he was not entirely happy off Island. In any event the arrangement worked well, since Jeff is also the producer of the Vineyard Players, a summer theater. For a good part of the spring, needed or not, he was drawing full pay (and as a union member he got plenty) to wander around his beloved Island and at the same time arrange his summer schedule.

William Blood of Darien, Connecticut showed up to play various people in various disguises. He is a playwright, member of the Screen Actors Guild, and his cousin conveniently owns a house in Edgartown where he had honeymooned in 1952. Craftily he borrowed his cousin's house (this was preseason) and settled in to play all the bit and extra parts he could get.

Edgartown also has two other summer-comers who turned into excellent actresses. One is Marion Moses, who unfortunately was off making a movie in Italy and the other is Diana Muldaur, who was working in a television series, "Born Free." Otherwise, it's a certainty that they both would've connived their ways into parts that would've given excuses to be on the Island.

Ruth Gordon, star of stage, screen and everything else she touches, owns a house in Edgartown, and although she was in rehearsal for "Dreyfus in Rehearsal" (a play which didn't make it) she agreed to take a bit part. When the day came, she was asked to play a dowager with a butler in the Fourth of July beach scene. She was to have sent the butler to check the water temperature and then hand her grandly into it. The part didn't appeal to her, perhaps because she was already on the Island and didn't need an excuse.

Actor Murray Hamilton arrived from New York to play the mayor, and it can only be surmised that he was not a country boy, since his first outdoorsy confrontation was with a skunk, which of all things, he kindly leaned down to pet. The intensity of the ensuing stench could only be compared to that being wafted from the Norton and Easterbrooks dock, where scup and other dead characters used for the chumming-for-shark scenes had been marinating in the sun.

Afterwards, Murray's comment was, "today everyone thinks he's a critic." But then, no one in his right mind would guess that the streets of Edgartown, up by the snappiest summer hotel, would tend to abound with foraging skunks after sundown.

The great news the second week of the Armada scenes was that the shark had arrived. Word had previously gone out along the eastern seaboard that *Jaws* needed a shark, so there had been considerable sea-searching for one, and an 11-foot tiger shark was turned up in Sarasota, Florida. It was promptly wrapped in salt and flown to the Island in its own private jet at the rumored cost of $12,000. The next day the Larsens, back from a fishing trip, reported that they had come through hundreds of them near the Island and could've brought back one for free.

With the arrival of the shark, sea-shooting was abandoned in favor of the dock, and the shark (dubbed Oscar by his exporters) was unpacked with all the excitement Christmas morning. 24 hours later no one cared if he ever saw another. For hours the shark was sung to, shot with guns, stabbed with arrows, sprayed with bug deterrent, hoisted by his tail (then his nose), washed with water, made-up and bloodied by Max Factor in conjunction with Del Armstrong.

Some of the old standbys, like Woodrow Wilson Sayre, Jini Poole and Alan Miller were wearing out there props and foul weather gear. There were additions in the crowd scenes of Carol Feiner, who should run a diner (but instead runs a French restaurant); everyone expected to see her filleting the shark. Then scores of Fligors showed up in assorted sexes and sizes. (This was the start of a precedent - scores of Fligors were always showing up).

All poked or pointed at the shark, which was worth pointing at, bristling as it was with arrows while smelly yellow goo used from the holes.

Henry Carreiro, playing one of the mad shark-snatchers in the posse, clowned his way through scene after scene, obviously having the time of his life. In fact, he had been such a ham that on occasion the directors had thought his lines funnier than theirs.

No sooner had he set eyes on the shark than he stuck his fingers into its heavily bloodied mouth and adlibbed. "One of our dental experiments." He thought a minute, couldn't resist and quipped, "Now we are going to do a fluoride commercial."

After the day's shooting, the by-now sagging shark was wrapped back in its salt, but for the next day's shooting it sagged even more. Amazingly, though, it smelled a good deal better as it had dried out.

All the make-up had caked to the extent that the face on the shark looked like plaster of Paris. Plenty of rumors were floating around about fake and mechanical sharks, and the poor tiger shark looked faker by the minute.

Since the shark was the center of action, that was the place to be, and Fanny Blair noticed how well the SAG members were at being in the center of the action.

At one point she was asked to walk down the dock right behind the police chief. "Goody," she thought. "I'll see myself on the screen," but during rehearsals a member of SAG oozed himself into her position so that by the time she reached the camera the director yelled, "Cut!"

Another huge SAG man turned out to be an expert at this and consistently got in front of Fanny so when she discovered him right beside the shark in the center of the shot, she snuggled up to him and said, "put your arm around me." He wasn't pleased; apparently, he didn't approve of scene stealers.

After the shark was finished with its moment in the sun it was left lying on the dock with a floppy expression on his wilted face, and with its make-up smeared.

Thereafter, more rumors circulated that *Jaws* had real sharks all over Edgartown Harbor. An off-Island newspaper published the story that the shark used in the dock scene had also been released in the harbor. This necessitated several calls of complaint, some saying it would have been wiser and kinder to shoot the shark and others saying, "wasn't that awful that the poor shark had been shot in the head?"

Post shark filming was back at sea where the winds gusted up to 40 knots, which made conditions dangerous as hell. Production was having problems with accurate weather reports and in desperation they telephoned their old reliable National Weather Bureau in Los Angeles. One can only wonder if the Bureau had ever heard of Edgartown, much less knew the weather conditions a continent away.

When the seas kicked up, plans were instantly changed. That afternoon the town was alerted to the fact that all was not normal. A band was playing in the distance, but it was the wrong time of year for bands. Those running errands to Main Street (which is the whole of Edgartown's downtown or business area… all of it contained in two blocks) were unsettled the find that *Jaws* had taken over the town.

The parade noises had been made by the Edgartown Boys Club Drum and Bugle Corps, and Jini Poole's son was a member of the corps. When Jini came home at five she found him flat on his back, "What's the matter with you?" she asked.

"Oh, mom," he moaned, "it was terrible. We stood there all day and roasted in the sun, and then they made us do it seven times! And each time someone did something wrong!"

The night before, Shari Rhodes had the idea that it would be very New England to hold a cake sale. She called Norma Bridwell, who had a difficult time organizing an instant benefit cake sale, which kept her women baking through the night. They made $50 on the sale as *Jaws* paid for the ingredients, although they were not allowed to meet the existing demand since the directors were afraid of running out of product before they had finished filming.

The Blairs, like most of the waterlogged extras from the Armada scenes, were delighted when the sea saga was scrubbed for the afternoon. After days of bouncing on the briny front sunup till sundown, they were able to tolerate the change. Other things needed to be done. So on their way home they stopped to do errands on Main Street and stepped back into *Jaws*.

They had parked their car just half a block away and instantly walked into all the excitement transpiring as arc lights and the drum and bugle boys toward the town. Fascinated, they watch, lingering and loitering like the rest of the pedestrians, as Fanny told Chuck, "It's fun seeing other extras making fools of themselves."

Brickmans of Martha's Vineyard had become Brickmans of Amity Island, the Edgartown Drug Company had become the JP Watson Drugstore, the country store had become a real estate office and a bike rental shop had appeared behind an instant picket fence which had also appeared, and Mr. and Mrs. John Coward's house (he's Coward Shoe) was dubbed the Amity Police Station. The sign hangs in the house to prove it.

Action ensued up and down North and South Water Streets at their intersection with Main Street, the busiest part of town, known as the Four Corners. 83 extras were walking their dogs, selling cakes, riding bikes and window shopping, all under bunting and a banner advertising the Amity Island Fourth of July Celebration and 50th Annual Regatta. Corny posters (such as Edgartown would never have) advertising the all-inclusive celebrations were displayed in shop windows.

Spectators accumulated with the extras, so it was hard for even the casting directors to tell them apart. There were also residents who accidentally got themselves trapped on the set and were trying to get off, or to the post office, by dodging in out of the crevices between buildings, keeping out of camera range.

Thoroughly sated with moviemaking, the Blairs returned to their car, but in its place was a huge double-barreled combination of mobile dressing rooms and comfort stations; the honey wagon. Chuck walked to the nearby police station (everything in Edgartown is nearby) but there was no one in the office; all the employees were naturally on Main Street watching. One such watching officer queried the rest of the "on-duty" constabulary with his walkie-talkie but no one knew about the car or, if they did, they didn't want to think about missing autos at a time like this. Offered a lift home, the Blairs passed the parking lot (again just off Main Street) which was loaded with cars, and there was there Buick.

They didn't know whether they were pleased or not. On one hand Clark would've been delighted if someone had stolen the

Buick which was so old that it no longer looked like a Buick; but on the other, they left all their uninsured foul weather gear and float coats in the car, and for a sailing family losing them would've been a catastrophe.

For once the weather had decided to cooperate and Main Street managed to look a bit like summer although the trees weren't quite out. In fact, the scene strongly resembled the real Fourth of July parade with people camping on the curb expectantly as they have for years waiting for the always-late parade to start. But there were bare limbs on the trees and no bare limbs on the people. It was too cold.

Arc lights were wheeled up and down the street as grips using double headed nails (so they would come out easily) put down tracks for the camera dolly, while behind them a cherry tree in full bloom in Leo J. Convery's yard did it's best to get into the act. This was not the only time that the blooming trees failed to respond to the timing of the plot.

Dotty Page had recently permanently moved to the Island. It'd taken a lot longer than she expected to get her Greek Revival house renovated, but at last the house and garden looked somewhat as she had hoped when she started.

Inside, things had been stashed "for now" in what later became known as the "for now" room, but it was time to get rid of the leftovers, so in Island fashion she held a garage sale. The sale went a lot better than she had hoped because the *Jaws* people descended like locusts. She never knew if they were buying souvenirs or, as Westerners, a heritage they didn't have, or as play caters for left behind wives.

"Anyway," said Dotty, "they spent an awful lot of money. One man bought a mirror for $50 and they paid $100 to have it crated and shipped."

While buying, they became enchanted with the Page garden, alive with blooming rhododendron, and conspired to use it as background. Like everyone else who wanted something of "theirs" in that movie, Dotty didn't tell them that gardeners watching *Jaws* would know rhododendron didn't bloom in July. However, the bushes never made it to stardom because that night they were pureed to a non-photogenic pulp by a storm.

But the garage sale itself had made such an impression that when the assistant second director, Barbara Bass, saw the conglomeration of equipment on the scow concocted as a mothership for the special-effects crew out at sea, she said, "shit this looks like a garage sale."

So when a name was needed in a hurry for the registration Barbara's expletive stuck and the strange craft was given the stranger name S. S. Garage Sale.

EAST CHOP TO MENEMSHA

The movie production of *Jaws* continued to roam the Island in much the same manner as a touring medicine show, playing in each of the Island's towns.

The early part of the last week in May they were at the Zinn house on East Chop, a point of land jutting into the sound from the town of Oak Bluffs. The name Chop derives from the fact that there are a pair of these juttings and to some ancient soul they resembled the chops (not the jaws) of an animal.

The house had been rented from Mrs. Earl F. Zinn with the condition that *Jaws* would redecorate parts of it for the movie and, if Mrs. Zinn wasn't pleased, *Jaws* would again redecorate ot the way she wanted. The house, used for a bedroom and dining room scene, is a typical shingle style Victorian summerhouse perched on tiptoes overlooking a placid expanse of blue (which can also be gray and dangerous) called Nantucket Sound. On a clear day you can see forever, but in fog and storms you can't see across the road.

This road, like all Island thoroughfares, was neither thorough nor fair, and certainly not designed with Universal trucks in mind. Needless to say Universal brought its usual clutter of paraphernalia and congestion.

Suddenly, and in no understandable way, the congestion increased when the entourage of encamped trucks and attendant confusion was enhanced by a house which seemed to prowl the streets with human intelligence. Slowly it encroached on the hub of action. The sidewalk superintendents thought it was part of the opus and, what's more, the opus did too.

As later discovered, this was the Sherman boathouse being moved in traditional Island manner to a new location, blocking the traffic as only a house moving can. The best laid plans of *Jaws* were hampered and did not improve when the boat house finally settled on an empty lot in front of the Zinn set. The young, educated Californians were (to say the least) surprised since was their first encounter with the maneuverability of New England houses. Granted, grips and set designers can do this sort of thing, but here was someone stealing your thunder and doing it for real, plunking a house right in front of them, ruining their view and continuity. You can't make a movie with the now you see at night own house in your foreground.

Jini Poole was stand-in for Lorraine Gary, who played the police chief's wife and as such, this was supposed to be her house. The writers weren't very pleased with Lorraine for some reason and kept writing her out of the script little by little so that each day there was that much less of her.

Jini didn't really have time to do this, and she knew it was nasty hard work but she wanted to see how the director worked with the stars. She had already seen how the assistant directors worked with the extras. So she crouched behind a chair for hours and was rewarded. The writing in the script was barely keeping pace with the filming, and at this point had even been outpaced, which was why Steve asked his actors to improvise.

"This is something very worthwhile," said Jini later, "and these people were good at it.

There were lighting problems with the small kitchen and a narrow passageway into it, so Jini had to stand for what seemed like an eon, and she realized that as far as the crew was concerned, she was only a warm body. It was, "move over here sweetie," or "down a bit honey," but never a name. Yet after a few days absence from the set, she was a long-lost friend, greeted by, "where you been sugar?" Or "why'd you desert us?"

Roy and Lorraine were filmed coming down an outside staircase after the scene was shot, as all others, over and over. Jini couldn't keep her eyes off Roy and wondered why until she realized each of his movements had been so well thought out and pre-planned as a series of poses that continued all the way down. "I do my homework," he told Jini.

This was apparent the way he shot off in the police car, swinging wide around the corner. Steve didn't like his hasty approach and Roy looked hangdog. "I thought you'd like it that way," he mumbled.

Parked outside at the Zinn house was French chef and author Tre Morse, and photographer Kathareen Tweed. They were there with her Yorktown Terriers and sat for two days, waiting. Then Steve decided that Yorkies were too nervous and used his own water spaniel.

When Jini decided to go elsewhere Fanny Blair took over as stand-in and for three days she mostly sat outside on a stool. "They only used me 25 minutes and standing under those lights I thought I was going to burn up, but I'd rather been burned and bored and on the inside then on the outside not knowing what was going on."

Carl Gottlieb, who was writing the script as they went along, popped out of the house to ask Fanny, "what kind of fish do young boys catch around here?" "Scup, I guess," replied Fanny, and learned that scup was inserted into the script. Rick Dreyfuss, playing the oceanographer (who should have known better" kept pronouncing it "scaup."

One of the days when she was sitting on her stool, Richard Zanuck brought Robert Shaw to the set and was introducing him. Fanny was intrigued that as of this late date he still had no idea what kind of character he would be playing and his valet was unpacking toupees and beards as fast as he was trying them on.

Fanny watched with appreciation since this was why she was sitting on the stool.

Inside the Zinn house she noticed that treasured beach plum blooms had been picked as a floral centerpiece. "You don't want to use these," she criticized. "No one is allowed to pick them." "No one will know," replied an art director. "What do you mean 'no one will know?'" gibed Fanny. "Lots of people are going to see this movie, aren't they?" This was her first experience with what the Islanders were to say all summer: "They just didn't listen."

The shooting and the house moving continued to coexist, with each crew fumbling its way through the other, not knowing who belong to what, and then they all evacuated at once.

Filming next moved to Harthaven where artist Douglas Prizer was the only resident to give permission for his beach to be used. For his courtesy he gained a dock. Part of the dock was built to break-away, but there was still enough left for him to keep. It was painted gray and up close looked like a stage setting, but from back where the clump of crew tangled with the electric cables it looked ancient and well weathered.

Trucks lined the two-lane Oak Bluffs-Edgartown Road out front, and clogged the drive, while the bluffs became bleachers. Shari Rhodes had goofed on this one. Actually, the characterizations were all right, just the names caused confusion. From 200 paces or 100 yards over water, or over infinite space through walkie-talkies, their names made more confusion than the directors needed.

Ed Chalmers and Bob Chambers, two Island day-players, shift onto the dock in the dead of dark (it was broad daylight, but the photo lab would fix that) and attempt to hook the shark for the reward. Instead, the shark made off with most of the dock, with the men in the drink. Thereafter the dock showed a tendency to follow Chambers or Chalmers -whoever it was - as he swam for his life.

The filming of this spectacle of idiocy was done from the dock (pre-shark) while enough of it was still there, and from the City of Chappaquiddick, a small ferry reconditioned by *Jaws*. A fleet of five boats stood by offshore connected by walkie-talkies to one another, the shore, in the main office back in Edgartown, and a bullhorn roared extra expletives. Lynn C. Murphy's high-powered fishing boat stood by (he'd at last found a job) with a battery of specially designed winches trailing off her stern. These winches were to pull pieces of dock, shark fins (or tails) people or anything else which might need submersive towing.

Occasionally these winch cables tended (as have all marine cables for a century) to get wrapped around propellers, wrapping up production for vague periods of time, while the office back in Edgartown grew impatient.

Only a photographer would understand why lights were needed in sunlight when it was supposed to be night, but needed they were, and since the filming was out in the water, so were the lights. Gaffers and special effects men encased in wetsuits spent most of the three days up to their necks in water, along with the electric cables. One slip on the slippery bottom at the wrong moment and, what with saltwater being such an excellent conductor, and 2000 watts in a cable, the spectacle would've become even more brilliant.

Police were everywhere. Neither of Mr. Prizer's neighbors was at all approving of this little gathering and they didn't want it to overflow on their land, so on the boundary sat the Oak Bluffs police, getting paid plenty, enjoying a few early spring days in the sun amid pretty young girl spectators who seemed to be allowed to trespass where they please, and growling at members of the operation who dared cross the invisible lines.

Actually, police were getting to be an Island problem since those in the movie were uniformed exactly like the Edgartown constabulary and suddenly there seem to be endless police. One intent on a misdemeanor must first peer around the officer, searching for considering what was going on their shoulder patch which either read Edgartown (for real) or Amity (for fake.

Considering what was going on at the Prizer place, on the beach, on the dock and offshore, the main road was pretty stable, just a few mammoth trucks, a few extra police talking to loitering Teamsters, and an assortment of spectator vehicles. Darting about were green station wagons was JAWS on their windshields, bringing off-Island reporters, actors, Shari Rhodes with her bag and pencils, or public relations man Al Ebner, to check on what the reporters were learning.

Through this mélange were black enameled men crossing the road to their trucks either for equipment or to change in and out of their wetsuits. *Jaws* needed lots of wetsuits and would need more before the summer was out. Production had tried to order them through Island stores, wanting to be kind to the natives, but by this time many of the Islanders were onto what they thought was a good thing. Assuming they had it made, they charged plenty and Universal found the suits could be brought in by jet from California for $60 less apiece.

Hotel living was expensive for the crew although they were paid a subsistence expense. Living in a hotel meant they had to eat out, and few places were open in April, not to mention that hotel rooms are notoriously dull and town bars have only seasonal licenses and must remain closed for six months.

Food was a serious problem. Granted they all got a good hot lunch every day, but it was still expensive eating in restaurants and they were used to places like McDonald's, the type of eatery Edgartown just does not have.

Several men found a two-room with kitchen apartment to share and were told it would be $250 a week. "Why?" they gulped, "this is out of season!" The current answer from the owner was, "Listen, I've heard you people are spending $30,000 a day on the Island and I want my share." One of the electricians wanted to buy a skivy shirt, and found a cost just twice as much as for the same thing in California. "For Christ's sake, why twice as much?" he asked. "Well, we've got a short season here and have to make it while we can." "Yeah, but this isn't summer." "I know, but we can't just lower the prices in winter." "I've never met anyone like you Islanders," the electrician threw back over her shoulder as he departed shirtless. "You even rob each other!"

Nurse Helen Jackson had been on location many times before, often in remote places like the wilds of Mexico or Alaska. She's a grandmother to whom home is a fancy anchored trailer (which he calls a mobile home) surrounded by shuffleboard, tennis, golf, swimming pools, club rooms and regulations about children and clotheslines.

She had learned not to live alone on location if she could help it and fortunately can do anything in a kitchen and loved doing it. She and a group which knew about her culinary achievements rented a house on School Street in the heart of the summer community and she was ecstatic.

"Everything's there," she reported. "I've never been in such a house. Usually, we're lucky to get a stove, much less blenders and nutcrackers."

Nutcrackers are a necessity on Martha's Vineyard in the heart of the lobster eating country, and the Californians made up for the deprivation at home. Along with the standard question about what the weather was going to do next, Islanders were often asked, "how long does lobster keep?"

Clam chowder is another culinary product peculiar to New England and Barbara Bass spent all summer trying to get one member of the crew to try it. Of course, he wouldn't until the last minute, and then couldn't get enough.

Seafood, particularly the lobster, came into Edgartown by way of Menemsha at the other end of the Island where Universal had built a house. It'd taken Joe Alves just a half an hour to draw the original plans, which were a composite of the Old Sculpin Gallery tower at Edgartown, built by the boat builder Manuel Swartz, and the Black Dog restaurant in Vineyard Haven, which was itself a replica of something, and the roof pitch of the Island fishing shanties.

Menemsha is a strange spot. The town, if you want to exaggerate by calling it town, is situated at the end of a creek, bordered on one side by the creek-caused swamp, backed by a hill on the inland side which is encrusted with summer cottages, and on the other sides are Vineyard Sound and a dashing spirited channel with a whipping tide in from the Sound to Menemsha Pond.

The few extant fishing shanties crouch on the east side of the channel with the docks, anchorage and red topped Coast Guard station, while across the narrow channel there is nothing. Flat and sandy lies what should remain a desolate remote land, belonging to the gulls and heron.

This is where Joe Alves wanted to build the house for Quint, the shark hunter. Quint, unwashed and unwanted, a cruel weirdo surrounded by myths and macabre stories, would not have neighbors and belonged on the uninhabited side of the channel. He was an outcast and well he should have been, but the desolate dunes belonged to the Town of Gay Head and in no worked on were the selectmen going to let anyone; Joe Alves, Universal or the whole Hollywood industry build in the gallery. It was a wise decision, since the breeding birds wouldn't have liked Quint either.

Instead, an empty lot was found at the head of the wet basin and *Jaws* posted a bond of $100,000 ensuring the return of the property to its original state by June 15. The studio had hoped to build a house which could be sold, thus retrieving some capital; instead, this one was built in pieces, some of it in Edgartown, assembled on the site, and returned to Edgartown where parts of it were used for reshooting.

During construction, enthusiastic officials of Chilmark got into the act, insisting that the building conform to the town's new building codes, while Albert Sylvia, who was doing electrical work in the house next door to supply current for the building tools, had to conform to the new electric codes.

When the house was finished Joe Alves had done such a great job that not only did the house belong, but it looked as if it always been there - and it often had to be pointed out to residents (who should've known better) as the house that *Jaws* built.

It's instant "weather" in the form of gray paint made it look generations old and the design, with red peeling tower, was such an addition that after all the furor the town fathers wanted it to remain and people were trying to buy it. However, the selectmen had driven a hard bargain and now, at the head of the basin, there is an empty sandlot with blowing candy bar wrappers and paper cups.

Jini Poole, whose real home port is Menemsha, came down to view the house and nearly threw her arms around Robert Shaw, who was leaning against it. He had so assumed the pose and character of an Islander that she thought he was an old friend.

Craig Kingsbury had been in part responsible for this, since had he been an actor, he would've been perfect for the part of Quint. He was therefore Shaw's template, and tapes were made so Shaw could study Craig's lingo.

The house was Quint's private slum area, where he dwelt, dissected marine creatures, docked his strange craft – Orca - and was surrounded by a magnificent gun collection (borrowed from Islanders) and an impressive array of teeth (still in shark jaws) brought from California (thank God they weren't local). Below, and in the process of being dissected, was a killer whale made of Lord only knows what, but it certainly wasn't made from what the Lord makes them. There were complaints to the natural resources officer, Paul Hotz, about the whale; scientists aren't for killing them and neither were the little old ladies in sneakers.

Quincy boat, tied to the dock, resembled something which should have remained 20,000 leagues under the Sea, and after construction by Universal was carefully painted with dirt.

Shooting was not done consecutively because Production wanted to get the Menemsha scenes over and back from processing in time to do any retakes before the lease (or the $100,000) was up on the 15th.

The first day on the set was a sunny warm Saturday, (the first of the year) so there was a "hi, ho, come to the fair" atmosphere, as verandas, porches, docks and hilltops were usurped for peanut galleries by the ever-gaping populace, and during off moments people toured the set as if it were the Louvre, climbing the tower, oohing at the guns and sticking their fingers in the sharks' teeth.

Instinctively, everyone seemed to know this was where the action was, so even New Yorkers were on hand. Mrs. David Brown, who is Helen Gurley, the editor of *Cosmopolitan* magazine, came to sit enthroned on a hastily improvised bleacher while chatting cozily with Steve Spielberg, heads together in the shade, so that it almost looked clandestine.

Robert Riger perched on a railing and photographed Robert Shaw in a scene aboard the Orca. It was done again and again. "Does this director realize what he's doing?" Bob asked. "Every time you repeat the scene Robert Shaw gets worse. Can you introduce me to someone who knows something about this?" Bob asked the Girl Photographer, "I want to hire Shaw for a movie."

"You won't get him," she answered, "he's trying to get out of the country - fast so he won't get caught for U.S. taxes."

Robert Shaw was beginning to improvise in the cockpit on the Orca, and Tom Joyner bellowed, "Cut!"

"I've never heard that before," said Steve. "I like it. Leave it."

Fanny Blair was back, sitting on her stool in front of Quint's house this time. She offered to give Sheri Rhodes a lift to Menemsha, but Shari had declined. "I'd love to, but I'm not allowed to, I have to go with Transportation."

AMITY? TOWN HALL

Disjointed, *Jaws* continued on its way filming, jumping about with different people as extras, and at different sites, so that surprise coups were constantly arising and those on the outside never knew what would happen (often neither did those on the inside). As with a forest fire, trucks and crew popped up hither and unexpected yon.

Every afternoon at 4:30 Steve Spielberg would confer with Barbara Bass about the next day's shooting and she in turn would get in touch with the casting offer via her ever-present walkie-talkie so that casting director Shari Rhodes and her crew could get on the phone collecting extras. If a person was home to answer the phone, he got the job; if he wasn't no second call was usually made unless that person was an absolute necessity.

The word was out that extras would be needed for the day after the filming was finished in Menemsha, so the front door stoop at the production office in Edgartown, where the call sheet was glued, was besieged by hopefuls.

Nevertheless, it was a surprise to the Island when one morning the Edgartown Town Hall was usurped. Main Street traffic not only slowed, but there was a definite pause – for - *Jaws* as drivers and their dogs (always in the front seat) ogled for all they were worth. 30 extras, Islanders all, served as "atmosphere." They at first stood around drinking coffee on the sidewalk, often spilling into midstreet while the scenes, as usual, took forever to set up, than alternately packed themselves in an out of the Town Hall on cue.

The 30 extras were turned loose in the narrow hall to point at the bulletin board and show excitement about the announced reward for the extermination of the shark. The hall got pretty noisy and narrow, so the fake mayor suggested moving into the selectmen's office, and the camera backed down the hall followed by the

30 arguing people while a Jack-in-the-Box arrangement of heads kept popping out of various town offices to see what was happening.

Needless to say, officialdom gave up any thought of concentrated work while grips and gaffers changed lights, reflectors, or the still photographer, Louis Goldman, tried to photograph the stars with their heads in the jaws of the shark - with teeth.

The town hall's own ceiling lights had been removed by Albert Sylvia so that new ones with higher voltage could be installed to hold high-powered photo floods, but something was dreadfully wrong and the fittings kept blowing the bulbs, which would be changed only to blow out again. This delayed shooting and the place was getting hotter by the watt.

In the selectmen's office sat the selectmen and the mayor, a bit scrunched since Edgartown does not have a mayor. Robert Carroll and Cyprien P. R. Dube, as former selectmen, had been this route before, and Alfred Wilde, playing Selectmen Keisel, turned out to be the director's pet since he'd spent many years in amateur theater.

Packed into the selectmen's office were the cameras and their crews, the selectmen and the 30 extras, the latter arguing and yelling which they had done in this room many times before. Then into the bedlam, unnoticed, stalked Quint. Robert Shaw had the character down pat and the man he portrayed was horrid. He bartered and threatened the town into hiring him for too much, and then slimed his way out.

Mrs. Robert G. Potter, Jr. was trying to do some planning board work, but her head kept popping in and out along with the rest. She was intrigued with Robert Shaw and could in no way believe that this grimy, greasy, surly fisherman (with an accent to match) was the same person she had seen as a comparatively dignified Henry VIII in *A Man for All Seasons* (1966).

The actors were inside or out, mostly packed in the selectmen's office, leaving little room for the functioning camera. Extras on the right side of the room would be sent out so the camera had room to photograph the left side and vice versa. Over and over the same action would be taken as the camera changed angles or lenses.

The room contained a few small nine lights (so called because there are nine lights with reflectors on a stand) and reflectors, but Production realized that the low-ceilinged room could not hold the mass of humanity and also the arc lights, so a large platform had been built for the latter outside, leaving them to peer like Cyclops's into the office windows.

Meanwhile, the Rolly Harper crew of two was getting lunch in the parking place and rushing fresh coffee, cocoa and pastry across Main Street to the arcade in front of the cheese shop. This was for the paid "loiterers" and no doubt some who weren't. They had fruit juice and soup in the afternoon and one could've gotten fat, courtesy of *Jaws*, with little effort. As a matter of fact, this did happen to some of the actors but not to Roy Scheider, to whom it could never happen.

For added atmosphere members of the high school band were "loitering" all morning. They were to have been seen outside the selectmen's office windows, but the shot would not work because the Town Hall still had storm windows up.

Mr. and Mrs. James B. Reston – he's of the New York *Times* - and they are both of the Vineyard *Gazette,* flew in that morning and promptly investigated Main Street. One look, and Sally Reston tore back to her house around the corner for her camera. Therefore, she had fun.

While Robert Shaw was on the set (stars aren't like the extras who have to "loiter") all the scenes were shot without keeping him waiting, which meant moving the lights, cameras and action back onto Main Street for his arrivals and departures. This entailed blocking the slow flow of traffic and using the extras as atmosphere to populate the town. Some walked and peered in windows, others curbed their dogs, while the Girl Photographer, by now recruited, had the joy of biking up Main Street the wrong way, a lifelong ambition.

Tre Morse, minus her Yorkie, was with her daughter, Carol Feiner, and since they had a lot to talk about, they had decided to serve as extras and get paid for spending a happy two days chatting and lunching. As street atmosphere (still chatting) they sat on a low wall. In the town hall they ended up in center-stage doing a good job and still talking.

Arthur Young, a jolly innkeeper with one gold earring and one red beard, was preceded everywhere by his lime green sweater, a combination making them easy to spot on the screen.

Jini Poole, on the edge of the town hall scene, expected to be telling her friends to look for the shadow under the radiator because, "that's mine."

Stephen Carey Luce, the Island's most prosperous banker, was a Town Hall extra with a prominent seat in the front row. But he got mighty bored with all the hang-ups, and the feeling he was not accomplishing anything got so overpowering that he drove back to Vineyard Haven to do some work. The still photographer had Polaroids of what was where, and who stood where, so that everything can be gotten back into the exact spot. Then suddenly in the afternoon Mr. Luce turned up missing. Since he had been in the previous shots he simply had to be in the next ones, but where the hell was he?

That hue and cry was out, town office telephones were requisitioned but no Mr. Luce, so the lights, cables and action were moved to something else until Mr. Luce returned, which (having finished something more worthwhile) he did.

"Dinner parties be damned," said the directors, and worked the extras from 6:30 that morning until 8:00 that night, then called them back at the same ungodly hour for another round the next day. Andy Stone tactfully gave them the word.

"Congratulations," he began, "you have all established yourselves, wear exactly the same thing you have on, you girls do your hair the same way, and be back here at 6:30 in the morning."

The same clothing down to the last detail must be worn for continuity, since the following scenes would be but a continuation of that same moment in time.

Once this continuity bit was really fouled up, Sheri Rhodes had a habit of roaming the streets looking for just the right faces to play her New Englanders, and she was not above snatching people off the street. On the afternoon they were shooting on Main Street a girl plotted by in her oldest clothes with no make-up and attracted the attention of Steve Spielberg, thereby landed herself a prominent part. The next day when she returned to finish the scene she was primped, powdered, and wearing an uplift bra. Sadly she had to be dismantled to her previous day's condition.

After another morning of shooting in the town hall and another lunch in the parking lot, the arc lights came off the platforms and most of the "too familiar" extras were dismissed. Those kept on took advantage of the chance to get into clean clothes while location was relocated to the newly created music store (which was normally a leather store).

All the big trucks which had been congesting Summer Street were congesting Dock Street on the harbor, and the plot called for Quint and his mate to show how much they were disliked in the town by dragging their nasty way up from the Orca at the dock to the music shop where they unsettled the populace and scared small boys.

Quint's mate had been hastily turned into Herschel West (with his miniature poodle, Topper) the minute Shari had discovered him at Menemsha, replacing a 20-year-old girl previously planned for the role.

Herschel was delighted to be in the plot. He and his dog were getting "actors" pay which was $135 a day, and the longer production dragged on the better he liked it. Later he would be transporting the generator on his own boat and at that point showed off a check for $1400 for the week.

No sooner had the cameras begun to roll than a fleet of 20 teenagers on bikes surged into range, look directly into the rolling camera and asked the soundtrack where the movie was being made. Unperturbed, Steve asked if they would mind biking past the camera again - this time on "action."

"Would they!" Delightedly they did it again and then biked off to discuss their good fortune.

During a moment when shiny cars parked outside were ruining the lighting inside, Robert Shaw, who had hitherto been spooky as Quint, grabbed an extras bike and, grinning happily beneath his grime, looped gaily through the extras, reviving his sense of humor.

While they were fiddling with the lights a man walked into the store, looked around the musical instruments, went outside, looked around, looked back at the shop, shook his head and finally asked where the leather store was.

No sooner were the cameras rolling in the music store that another stranger walked in and immediately asked to buy some sheet music. When the scene was finished the gaffers moved down to the Orca on the dock, and grips started to reconvert the music store into the leather store, when suddenly Steve came dancing back from the harbor singing, "The director doesn't know what he's doing," and the leather store, music stop, leather store was re-music shopped.

When the extras were dismissed that afternoon, the Teamsters lounging on their trucks looked sad. "Come back and see us," they pleaded! For this was to be the end of shooting on land for three weeks - the end of the medicine show atmosphere, the traipsing about the Island, the end of the colorful scenes that popped up unannounced, for the fleet was shipping out to sea.

SEA SAGA

The following day *Jaws* went down to the sea in ships, but it was hard to tell where there was the most water; above or beneath or falling.

Production expected to get the sea shooting over in three weeks. The middle of June was upon them, and they were still hoping to leave by the first of July. Little did anyone dream the time would be closer to three months. So they worked through the torrential rains.

For the second day's sea shooting the wind blew and the crews, still damp from the previous deluge, were back out there but this time they got wet from the other direction; spray, spume, and leaks.

The weather had been cold, windy, and sloppy for the Armada scenes when the little boats had avoided swamping only by excellent seamanship and a raft of luck. This was worse, real stormy stuff; and most of the six boats were overloaded without proper safeguards. Shooting was done off Harthaven, that magic spot where *Jaws* had first wanted to do all its filming but, having been denied the use of the private harbor, they were working outside in wild water.

The old ferry scow, the City of Chappaquiddick, was used as the electric barge. She had been built in the 30s by Manuel Swartz for Tony Betancourt, was the first powered car ferry to Chappy and was one of those everyone-said-its-couldn't-be-done things, a folly ferry. But she had been done and was now trying her darndest to survive. She was so loaded with arc lights, cables, nine lights, reflectors, crew and paraphernalia stacked on her flush deck that walking her length, even in a calm, was a nightmare.

Although everyone, camera and lights, must've been flying about in an uncomfortable sort of way, those in authority didn't respect the sea enough to know that what they were doing had reached the danger point. The good old City of Chappaquiddick let them know.

Eventually even non-seamen could notice that their electric barge was rapidly losing freeboard, working hard in the swells, and her pumps, inadequate to begin with, had clogged.

This alarming situation necessitated considerable communication over the walkie-talkies located in every boat captain's hip pocket. Lynn Murphy listened aboard his boat in nearby Oak Bluffs Harbor and bounced out to have a look. Meanwhile, someone had pushed the panic button and notified the Coast Guard that six boats were sinking. That's a lot of boats to handle at one time so the 82-foot Point Jackson, and an air sea rescue helicopter (to lower pumps), were dispatched.

Before they arrived, it was discovered that no boats were actually sinking, although the City of Chappaquiddick undoubtedly had it in mind. She was chaperoned to her birth in Oak Bluffs by Lynn since there was a question whether her consumption of salt water would reach her engine before she reached the harbor. Fortunately, the good old screw (which had never been so far from Edgartown, all of 6 miles) wallowed back under her own power and stiff upper lip.

Herschel West, no longer needed to play Quint's sidekick, was using his boat to carry the generator in a crate perched on the gunnels. Under normal conditions, which means sanity, Herschel would never have overloaded his boat with a top-heavy crate to begin with, but his appetite had been wetted for *Jaws*. Finally, boatman that he was, he yelled, "I'm going in!"

So, with the generator departing, there was little else to do but fire him or follow him, and they decided to follow.

None of the harborside residents thought much of it when the boats came in. The time was 12:30 and any Islander can tell you this is the noon hour, the lunch hour to the always have a big party and then come join you the rest of America, when the big helicopter whirled in low, trailing the Point Jackson, residents were alerted and switched on their ever present scanners and citizens band radios in time to hear Chief Jesse Oliver ask the police cruiser to go to the assistance of *Jaws* at the Yacht Club. This, in the ears of listeners, spelled an emergency, but it wasn't. The chief, undoubtedly having heard about the tyro tars connected with *Jaws*, was expecting the worst.

Once safely tied up at the Yacht Club (and a stranger craft has never laid there) the Orca promptly lost her rudder. Then the camera boat, Scup Bucket, approaching the dock disclosed the fact that she either wouldn't or couldn't reverse, nearly de-docking the town. Later diagnosis disclosed driveshaft inefficiencies.

In the interim of non-navigability the Coast Guard gave *Jaws* a tongue lashing, personnel were driven halfway back to Oak Bluffs for lunch at the Bend in the Road, the City of Chappaquiddick used the Coast Guard pumps, the rudder was replaced on the Orca, the driveshaft was tampered with, the wind dropped and at 4:31 the flotilla was re-floated and headed back to Harthaven, albeit Scup Bucket was noticeably slower.

That was Monday, and by Tuesday night there was evidence that *Jaws* was in trouble again. The harbor front was a blaze of light and perched right in the center of it, high and dripping on the Norton and Easterbrooks dock, was the Orca.

The saga of the Orca isn't too sane. She was an old boat, bought not too cheaply, and navigated from Boston to Martha's Vineyard by Nelson Smith. Universal, in its usual impatience, was wondering what was taking so long and Nelson reported back, "She's the slowest damn son of a bitch I have ever been on. I had to keep going over to the side of the Cape Cod Canal to let the rowboats pass."

Immediately upon arrival she was put into the hands of Joe Alves. Non-nautical Joe had been searching for books on boats, learned nothing apparently, and re-created the Orca on a rather good-looking Nova Scotia lobster boat hull. Off come her superstructure to be replaced by a super-superstructure, topped by a flying-flying bridge. Her old wooden hull was not re-planked or caulked but four large eye bolts were screwed into what would proximate her four corners had she been anything but a boat. Peter Eldridge, who worked on her, was against those bolts and proved to be right.

Peter was a good boat builder and the son of an architect, so he had grown up with wood, creation and boats, but he was having problems. He didn't know whose orders to follow or understand the levels of command. "It was a hilarious April. I'd start something and the next official in the shed would cancel it and tell me to do something else, then the next official would tell me it was all wrong and to do it over. Finally, Joe Alves said, 'you do it your way.' There was some sanity in the shed then since there were only four of us working but eventually there were forty."

As the Orca got taller with all her super-superstructure, Peter knew she was going to be like a rolling ball without 4000 pounds of lead ballast. Production wasn't sure they wanted any ballast, so harangue ensued. Then, at 11:55, they agreed and wanted the led by noon.

Peter and his coworkers had some, bought some more and borrowed 1000 pounds from Michael Jampel, a Vineyard Haven dentist who planned to use it for the walls of his X-ray room.

After several hundred pounds of lead had been loaded aboard the Orca, Production changed its ever-changing mind and decided to weight her down was cement - it would be cheaper. Thereupon 40 bags replaced the lead, to the tune of Peter explaining, "You're not going to like this - those bags will take up too much room and ride too high. The weight has to be low to be effective."

Then inevitably someone changed their alleged mind so the cement was off-loaded, but in the process of its two-way journey, fingers punctured the bags and, of course, the Orca leaked. "WHAT A MESS!" remembered Peter.

Jim Fargo decided that Universal would rent the lead, which he figured they would need for three weeks to complete the sea shots, and the charge was to be $.40 a pound for the first and third weeks and half-price for the second week. But then the three weeks turned into ten and Jim Fargo was replaced as Unit Manager by Bill Gilmore, who didn't see the humor in renting the lead, waxed stubborn, and refused to play. "This is how wars start," thought Peter.

What's more, during the 10 weeks of shooting weights would be needed to replace lost anchors or to hold or balance an assortment of things, so gradually much of the lead disappeared.

Finally, at the end, Peter was called to, "come get your God damned lead!"- what was left of it.

Shortly thereafter he happened to see a collection of lead in Roy Campbell's locker. "That's Dr. Jampel's lead," he said, "where did you get it?" "I fished it off the bottom, but if you want it you're going to have to pay me salvage," replied Roy.

The Orca's super-superstructure was painted seasick green, piped with stale-blood red and the rest was glass.

"What you think of her?" Freddy Zendar asked the Girl Photographer when he first tied her up at the Norton dock.

Girl Photographer was Edgartonian enough to know about boats, but she wasn't sure this was a boat. "She looks kinda odd, more like a stage setting then a real boat."

"Yes," replied Freddy, who acted as the *Jaws* nautical consultant. "It's all that glass. It wouldn't make sense to have that much at sea, it's dangerous. That's Hollywood, everything has got to be bigger than life. Come look."

The strange craft was in the throes of being made stranger. Beautiful sennit work had been plaited over her pulpit and shark jaws gnashed from the flying bridge, a windicator of small shark tales spun from her masthead and painters were painting her, not with pain, but with dirt. A man in a dinghy started to screw on handmade iron letters proclaiming her as ORCA. (Later, Governor Francis W. Sargent would christen her).

"Do you like 'em?" asked Joe Alves as he cruised up to inspect the work.

"Yes, but they're pretty fancy for the likes of that boat," said someone.

"They're supposed to have been made by Quint, he loves his boat."

"But they're going to rust like hell when they get out there in that saltwater."

"That they will," said the grinning Joe, and one could see his delight as he pictured the blood-red from the rusting letters dripping down the Orca's transom.

But here was Joe's pride on the waves in the dark. It seems that when she had lost her rudder the previous day, the restraining cables had not been replaced and, while in reverse, the rudder had slammed into the propeller. This promptly attempted to munch into the rudder, which refused to be munched, so the result was a bent prop.

The old tub (rather, the Orca) vibrated more than necessary after that. *Jaws* divers went down to appraise the mess and she was about to be hauled by Larry Grant, owner of the Chappy ferry, using a sling and the Yacht Club hoist on the Coal Wharf, when Bob Carroll just happened on the scene. Bob had once been a fisherman (what Islander hasn't at one time or another?) and realized that picking the old tub (there's that word again) up by a sling would break her back. He swears he was not actually drumming up trade for his boat yard when he suggested using the yard's hoist and doing it right

This was a business where no time may be wasted, so the big arc lights and generators were shipped over and the dock was lighted as never before while uncomplainingly everyone went to work on top of a hard day of work. This was Hollywood at its best.

Jon Ahlbum, who had been an extra in the Town Hall scenes wearing a shirt advertising his garage, appeared to change the prop, (fortunately, just by luck there was a spare) and welders worked far into the night spraying the dark with their stars.

Long before sun-up, the Orca was back in the water looking as normal as she could, but there were those who would not forget her sitting on the waves dripping what looked like ink from her black hull while her blood-red sheer strips seemed to drip blood, making her eerie and evil.

"It could've been avoided," said Freddy Zendar. "I told 'em but they just don't listen."

About this time, Barbara Bass had lunch at the Black Dog in Vineyard Haven and thereby discovered (just by looking out the window) the tug White Foot. She came back charging in on Jim Fargo with the news. "There's a big tug over there that's just perfect for us, it can carry the generator. It has a galley and a big flat deck with a big crane and a bathroom!"

Jim wasn't impressed. Someone else had spotted the tug and he had already discovered the price was too high.

But the sea scenes weren't going well. One reason was that they didn't have nautical generators and when the boat rocked, all the oil went to one side, making for erratic function. Production was running behind schedule, so much so that it was finding problems multiplied by the beginning of the summer tourist invasion. At the same time, costs were rumored to be running well ahead of the projected estimate of $4 million. In fact, things had been going so badly they'd given rise to all sorts of rumors - that the movie could be called off; that troubleshooters had arrived to straighten the operation out; that the Mafia was involved, or that the film would be completed in Hollywood.

It was also rumored that the Screen Actors Guild was displeased with a large number of local extras being used in the picture. Since Guild members were paid more than twice what non-members got, and since Islanders looked a good deal more like what they were supposed to be - which was Islanders - and because getting Guild members to the Island was difficult, more Islanders were logically used as extras. But the Guild tended not to see it this way.

The weather was getting its two cents into the affair by behaving in an uncooperative manner the way Island weather always does in spring, so everyone was saying, "Why didn't they come in the fall - we have lovely weather. It's always wet and windy in spring?" Another case of not listening.

Once the filming offshore had commenced – horrors - it turned out that Robert Shaw got seasick, which encouraged others aboard the various boats to emulate him. Smelly chum, stashed aboard and ripening in the sun while waiting for its big scene, undoubtedly had some bearing on this, as did the hyperactivity of the sea.

Then, when more confusion wasn't needed, the Orca conked out. This performance was strictly superfluous ad-libbing, but Universal seemed to have picked a stubborn fleet of character boats; each with a mind of her own.

In the swirl of flying rumors, Jim Fargo, who was on his first movie of this size, was sent back to Hollywood ostensibly to cope with the unions, but actually he landed in Switzerland on another assignment, while his boss, William Gilmore, moved into run the show himself.

SHARK! SHARK!

The sharks were an opus all unto themselves, and there was chatter to the effect that when Roy Scheider began to realize that the shark was really the star of the movie, his whole personality changed.

He was right. No matter how you slice it, the sharks were not only the stars, they were prima donnas. Heretofore, Hollywood may have thought it had trouble with doting parents and child actors, temperamental female stars and top billing antics, but nothing - absolutely nothing - had equaled the sharks for temperamental fits and egotistical behavior. They needed constant care, either dental, dermal or cosmetic, and were tended by a crew of specialists in special-effects. Even with all this pampering, on several occasions they wandered off on their own and actually took out their orneriness by biting people.

It's no wonder that Roy felt upstaged.

The performing shark was an enigma since sharks don't perform on cue. In the beginning, shark expert Peter Gimbel, armed with photographers Ron and Valerie Taylor, went into the waters off Australia's Great Barrier Reef where the great white shark lurks with intensity. The idea was to collect miles of footage which could be inter-spliced through the movie, sprinkling it with sharks as needed.

That was great and the sharks turned out spooky his belt. However, the only shark which showed any interest in the man in the shark cage was not a 25 footer called for in the script, so a midget was sent down in a smaller cage and instantly the shark grew 20 feet.

That took care of some of the movie, but Mr. Benchley had created an exceptionally active shark and Universal had made him more active. He didn't just swim in the sea eating people at a leisurely rate, oh no, he entered lagoons, ponds, broke into shark cages, slunk through cocktail parties, towed docks and sank boats while his diet included not just people but dogs, rubber mattresses, children, chains, nude maidens (supposedly dragon fare) steak and tanks of oxygen.

Sharks aren't bright enough to be trained (plus having a slight tendency toward eating their trainers); however, they can be lured. But they will also lurk, pounce and be downright dishonest. Therefore, much to Joe Alves' chagrin, fake sharks just had to be used - but only as a last resort - and only when the real ones waxed uncooperative.

Absolutely ingenious mechanical sharks were therefore designed to look, feel and move like the real thing - intended to behave like the real thing - unpredictable. There's no record of one of them eating anyone, and no one turned up missing, but they sure pulled every other trick in the book and succeeded in scaring their caretaking divers half to death.

Robert Mattey, once of Disney Studios, was responsible for most of the creativity involved in the sharks, which came in two denominations; the sea- sled shark, which was designed to be pulled through many an interesting situation, and the platform sharks. These were little more than half-sharks, one to be photographed from the right and the other from the left. They were operated by a mammoth rig of construction steel cover with rubberized ocean bottom green paint. It is reputed to have cost $23,000 just to haul the rig and the sharks from California.

Apparently, the rig was severely shaken up somewhere along the 3,000 mile trek, because the hydraulic legs wouldn't work when it arrived. The rig was designed to be raised and lowered by compressed air, and could level itself on the bottom 23 feet down by its hydraulic legs. There was a sheave on top of the crane which pulled the sharks through the water, or raised them to leap on rowboats, cockpits, or people.

The sharks themselves were designed to wiggle where sharks wiggle and munch were sharks munch, involving a control panel and pressure gauges outdoing the proverbial cockpit of the B-29. Inside, the sharks were filled with 300 feet of multicolored intestines which were hoses bearing pneumatic pressure to control points.

When all this arrived there had to be places to put it, store it, work on it, and some places to stow everything while at sea. For this Universal obtained the use of some land on Oak Bluffs harbor which was promptly dubbed Shark City. It was here that the two dry-docks and the addition of an overhead platform, for the cameras to get a terns eye view of the ensuing drama, were built. Since the sharks are 25 feet long with about a 5 feet beam, their floating docks were huge things guaranteed to shock the un-expecting sailor.

A couple with two young children had driven from St. Louis to spend their first vacation on the Vineyard. (They should've known better). The trip with the wiggly children had been harrowing, and both parents were in a state of exhaustion when they camped on the after deck of the ferry Islander for the trip across the sound.

Just as they were nearing East Chop, one of the sharks was towed past. The woman blanched; speechless, she pointed the monster out to her husband, and he turned to the nearest stranger with, "W-w-what's that?"

The stranger, feeling somewhat the same way, replied that he thought "it might be a shark - and all of 30 feet. God, what a monster!"

This was said within hearing of the mother, who by now had collected her darlings into her lap and was shielding them from the sight. When the couple arrived at their inn the exhausted mother clutched her children as the father explained, "We won't be staying. This is a dreadful place!"

"Why?" asked the clerk.

"We've been misled to believe that our children would have wonderful safe beaches to play on."

"They will," replied the clerk.

"No, they won't, we love our children. Do you think we'd let them in the water with those sharks?"

It can only be hoped that after a good night's rest things looked brighter.

Shark City was where the S. S. Garage Sale was built. She was a nautical horror story and by rights she never should've been conceived or, once conceived, she should not have survived. Yet somehow, like the bumblebee, she made it.

S.S. Garage Sale was a large platform designed and built by Ralph Packer. She managed to stay afloat on barrels of air, while she got around (if you want to call it that) propelled by half-ton outboards. On the platform was a house with a gable roof and shark weathervane. Her exterior walls were sheathed in shiny black plastic which could be rolled up but never were except when she was under way. On the stern - or was it the bow (it was hard to tell) - was a console to operate the outboards and presumably steer the thing. But there was absolutely no way to see where it was going since the house with all its clutter was in front of the helmsman.

Abaft the console were the control wires, hoses, compressors and such which operated the motions of both the platform and sharks.

Inside were dressing rooms, so divers could change their clothes, and -wonder of wonders - a "head," which is what a "john" becomes when it goes to sea. Throughout, over, under, above and beneath were equipment, clothing, props, gear, wardrobe, diving equipment, tools, cameras, coffee urns, compressors, bus seats, stacks of plastic cups, hoses and all manner of special effects and diving gear. There were also teeth and scrub brushes, for the sharks face. It kept getting dirty.

The shark kept wearing out its skin in places which was replaced and patched after the rougher scenes. Teeth were another problem. It was soon learned by everyone on the set that a real shark has plenty of spares and only takes 18 hours to replace a lost tooth, or one that he leaves in the gunnel of a boat or someone's leg. The *Jaws* sharks did it faster and, what's more, had two types of teeth; plastic for munching on boats, barrels, shark cages, oxygen tanks or transoms, and rubber teeth for munching on people.

Stuntman Teddy Grossman came aboard the S. S. Garage Sale after a long stint with the shark and, pointing to the trickle of blood on his leg yelled delightedly, "Look, it bit me!"

No one had told him that they'd run out of rubber teeth and that there were some plastic ones in the maw.

Because Joe Alves had wanted so badly to do it for real he did not want the outside world to know that fake sharks would be used. Also, because many real sharks were used in the movie - and because the producers wanted moviegoers to enjoy the movie and not speculate on which sharks were fake and which were real - they intended to keep the mechanical sharks under wraps and away from prying lenses.

The sharks were therefore stored secretly in the loft over the Fuller Street boat shed and there were not many on the Island who did not know of their arrival. One of the first shark accidents occurred when Harold McGee of *Newsweek* came down for an interview with Steve Spielberg and collected a *National Observer* photographer along the way. Jim Fargo took both men up to see the sharks, asking that they not take pictures, but the *National Observer* got a scoop and published the first one. After that, a full-time guard was stationed on the loft, along with tempting signs reading, "Shark - No Admittance."

The guard should have remained there for most of the early summer, but somehow his schedule got fouled up. Everyone thought there was a guard on duty, but there wasn't, so until that was discovered half the populace - at their leisure - wandered in, Instamatics at the ready.

Along about the middle of June an Edgartown resident driving to Vineyard Haven spotted something fishy waving from the rear end of the truck. She followed it and landed in Shark City behind the first shark on its way to be launched. Photographers galore were attracted to the scene and asked not to publish the pictures. They promptly did.

Universal had been in such a panic to get the sharks East that they had never been tank tested. Brown and Zanuck had begged to have this done in California where, if they had not worked, they could've been fixed or amended, but no; East they came - virgin sharks all.

Into the sea went the maidens and then it was discovered that there was a difference between the studio tank water and Nantucket Sound - salt! It soon became apparent that circuitry sharks were susceptible to electrolysis- - - - Back to the drawing board.

About this time, it was the middle of June and the house that *Jaws* built in Menemsha was deconstructed in the nick of time, the $100,000 bond was saved and the building stored in the Fuller Street shed for occasional retakes. Production sighed with relief, but the residents of Menemsha missed their tourist attraction.

ON THE BEACH

When the sharks didn't work, and Robert Shaw returned to Canada, calls for help were directed to poor Sheri Rhodes who had been excused for three weeks and returned to Texas. She flew back, picked up her pencils and was instantly tying up the Harborview switchboard calling, "extra, extra." Beach scenes were imminent.

While she, Janice Hull and Jini Poole monopolized every phone they could get their hands on, a few Boy Scouts were dumped in the chilly harbor waters for a swimming meet, just so the officialdom of Amity Island could call them in or out of the water, depending on who was winning a political argument.

Without warning, the cameras and their merry crews descended on the Norton and Easterbrooks dock during the busy launching season. After several uncomfortable weeks of shooting on the high seas it must have been nice for the crews to have terra what's-its-name back underfoot.

One camera with a 500 mm lens was tripoded in the middle of the hoist while the Scouts swam through the harbor after a red rowboat leading them through an arrangement of international orange buoys which tended to drift off-station,

Only a small percentage of the populace was on hand to sidewalk-superintend since watching without benefit of 500 mm vision was inefficient.

Another camera was back at sea riding the Chappaquiddick ferry with its load of arguing officials, thus interrupting inter-Island transportation. Suddenly, to the consternation of the viewers and the waiting customers, Dick Hewitt took her off course and toured the channel at right angles to his usual run.

This was now the third week in June and Production let it be known that, no matter what the calendar said, it was about to be the

Fourth of July for the second time. In fact, it would be the Fourth of July for a week. Monday the Fourth. Tuesday the Fourth. Wednesday... All wrong, of course, since it was more like the first week of the Fourth, the second week of the Fourth, the third week of the Fourth...

Barbara Nevin, still having the time of her life working as secretary, took Bill Gilmore to a meeting of County commissioners, the conservation commission, selectmen of Edgartown and Oak Bluffs and the shellfish wardens of both towns. The idea was to get permission to shoot a few scenes in Sengekontacket Pond.

Bill Gilmore said that he hoped to get the beach scenes, the last shots on land, over within the week and be off the Island before the opening of the season at the end of the month. He added pensively that it would be painful if the production were to run over into the season, "at seasonal prices," for room and board.

On this occasion County Commissioner Shirley Frisch told him, "we hope you'll have a pleasant stay, we like the look of your money."

While the extras battened down for a nonstop Fourth, State Beach on the Edgartown-Oak Bluffs Road was readied with all possible dispatch and excess manpower.

The cabanas, bandstand, "closed" hotdog stand and penny arcade created an instant public beach.

Back into the sand went the arc lights, the track for the camera dolly and atmosphere. Atmosphere, Islanders soon learned, was people in the background doing what people would normally be doing in the background while the actors are acting up front.

The first day's shooting had a perfect day for the beach. Carol Fligor was there with her children or somebody's children (it's always hard to tell) holding a pre-Fourth birthday party with a big yellow cake. There were a few uneasy moments when, what with all the rehearsing and perpetually famished young, the cake consumption was too high and Tom Joyner had to yell, "No cake between takes."

The children were cooking hotdogs over a fire which, like all picnic fires, prefer not to burn and had to be coaxed into flare-ups by the special effects men who were cautioned not to burn down the cabanas.

During the usual number of numbing rehearsals and takes, Steve Potter's Labrador retriever was lucky. He got a stick thrown into the water for him to fetch. The more takes the better as far as he was concerned; he never had it so good. Later he was to be eaten by a shark, but he didn't know this then.

Much of the crew appeared in bathing suits and took the plunge between takes, creating some interesting moments among the gaffers who were working with 2000 watts dripping that ever conductive saltwater.

Pebbles at the water's edge were a problem for some tender feet after a winter in shoes, so soft sand had to be brought in to remake the beach, and that took a while.

Steve Spielberg had been doing some plotting and in off-hours dreamed up an impact-laden scene by having a zoom lens zoom away from Roy Scheider looking worried, while the camera dashed in on the dolly. Wham! The idea was great but took forever to explain and rehearse. Then seven takes were shot before everything was right with the sound, with the track, with the zoom, with the focus, with Roy, who has the kind of face which lends itself to problems and with the background, which tended to become cluttered with grips.

Every now and then there would be a great hiss of compressed air escaping from the S. S. Garage Sale anchored off Harthaven, as something went askew with the sharks, and this would foul the soundtrack. Four Lasers were trundled across the sand by frustrated grips who were there to build a fence but couldn't make hammer noises when the camera was rolling. A Laser, for the benefit of non-sailing lovers, has nothing to do with light application but is a small sailboat along the lines of a surfboard with ambition. The Warners had one, and that's how they all got into the movie.

The Warners were second-generation summer-comers. There was father Everett and young Everett, mother Elizabeth (Libby) and young Elizabeth (Betta) and Eleanor. They read about the excitement of *Jaws* in the Vineyard *Gazette* and were sorry school wasn't out so they could get down and watch. But then suddenly school was out, and *Jaws* was behind schedule.

The children had been embarrassed about applying for a job, but employing their boat at $10 a day was different. Everett (father) had not been well, so sitting on a beach appealed to him and he began to wonder if older men weren't just what Shari might be looking for. They were, as well as families, so Shari took the Warners en masse.

The young these days seem to be perpetually looking for jobs, but they were not what Shari needed. She needed families or men who would naturally be off on a real holiday, and most adult males were not available for a miserly $20 a day, especially when they heard they would have to bring their own lunches.

400 extra people were not only too many to feed, but 400 extras were too much for the honey wagon and Bob Calin, the operator who polished all its chrome wheels with daily devotion, was determined not to let 400,

sandy messes into his immaculate segregated four-holer comfort-station.

Therefore, four strange igloo-like restrooms appeared beside the road, where anyone using one had a horrid feeling that it was going to tip over, thereby catapulting his nakedness upside down on the highway, but that never happened.

Fanny Blair was besieged by her friends arriving for the summer, who knew she had "connections." Betty Dickinson wanted in, and obviously it wasn't for the $20 because her husband is Farleigh Dickenson. Crosby Foster, just finishing his first Island winter, asked for a part; Arthur Nicol wanted the fun. He should have been working for a good deal more, - painting – but this looked like a once-in-a-lifetime thing; artist William Abbe tried to charter Barbara Bass his old catboat, but found himself snagged by Shari instead

George Silva needed a between times job; the season still wasn't in full swing, but Cy Blackwell - as former Registrar of Motor Vehicles - was used to being in uniform and had time to have fun. Frank Murray, with a theatrical resume as long as his swimming trunks, wanted in, even though he would be committing daily from Falmouth on the Cape.

By now some of the families of the crew were arriving to stay or vacation. The Island weather was supposed to be improving into what a summer resort is famous for, so the families entered the melee on the beach along with everyone else who could get in.

Fanny Blair, still fascinated, was there as were others from the Armada scenes. Jini Poole couldn't resist either, and arrived with her whole family and proceeded to hold her daughter's 16th birthday party on the set.

The Warners happened to sit next to William Abbe and soon discovered (small world) that he now owned their old Rolls-Royce. Elizabeth (Libby) then discovered that Dionis Riggs, whom she had always wanted to talk to about Island history, was only two blankets away.

Maggie Moffett got interested in *Jaws* when she hitched a ride on one of the Universal trucks. "What do you think of our movie? Ready the kitchen" the driver asked his pretty passenger. "Not much," answered Maggie. "They won't give me a job."

Several days later, Maggie found herself sitting on Fourth-of-July-Beach in shivery winds, running from a shark in ice water and, after 10 hours of this (she admits she was out of condition), it was more than she could stand, and she quit, but not before she had met Steve Spielberg.

He plopped down next to her on the beach during one of those delays, and started giving her the usual line. When he left ten minutes later, cute gay Maggie had fallen in love and, when he left the Island three months later, she was still under the spell, although she had never spoken to him again.

Because she asked everyone about Steve, Maggie learned a lot. She had heard that he had come from a family which could afford to let him work on his dream of movies, she knew that he could afford nice clothes - like the blue jeans with zippers everywhere - and that he had rented a log cabin, had a cook and entertained members of the company for dinner which kept him out of the public eye and with his nose to the grindstone. She learned that Steve hated boats and didn't think too highly of helicopters, which he would be riding in the beach scenes.

When it was rumored in the fall that Steve might buy the log cabin, she was excited and when he didn't she was disappointed and so were a lot of others who liked having Hollywood in their midst.

"You know," said one Islander, "I used to think all those Hollywood people were a lot of kooks, but you know what - they're just normal people working for their living."

So, while the Islanders clamored to get into the movie and Robert Shaw sojourned in Canada (to the great regret of the Internal Revenue Service) the beach scenes were about the start, treating extras and residents to two weeks of experiences long to be remembered.

FOURTH OF JULY BEACH

Orange and white striped cabanas and a green and yellow bandstand rose like a mirage from the sea to poke flags and finials through the mists and emerge as Baghdad-on-the-Bay. Mythical, misty and miraculous, it was a pageant beneath the twisting terns, as the flags flew and the band played and the 400 arrived.

This was not a Fifth Avenue party of early 1900s and it wasn't that same 400 which spread itself and its lunch on the beach, but 400 who had come perhaps to be eaten by stray sharks. The 400, from all walks of Vineyard life, came for the day (even though it looked like rain). They brought their children, their mothers and maiden aunts, and enough paraphernalia for 800 people spending eight hours on the beach, rain or shine.

The beach seemed unnecessarily to be crawling with police. There were police borrowed from a nearby town (near Amity that is). Coast Guardsmen (fake), Amity police (fake), Oak Bluffs police (real), Edgartown police (ditto) and shark patrol, all duly uniformed, badged and pistoled at the hip. Half this constabulary was transported to offshore vessels in Chinese-drowning-party fashion, unbeknownst to the Coast Guard (real). Norton and Easterbrooks Nor'East launch was one of the craft, leaving touring yachtsmen with no way to get ashore. She was plastered with large red signs proclaiming that (like it or not) this was the Amity Harbor Patrol.

Eventually filming started, but not until after hours of rehearsing background action. Artist William Abbe haggled over the price of a shark book; Arthur Nicol hauled boats; the Drew family arrived from Brooklyn while Crosby Foster kept the peace and George Silva lugged shark repellent across the beach in unbending rehearsals and unending takes.

The principals arrived for a day on the beach about 10 times, William Abbe bought the book 10 times, the shark repellent was loaded on the boat 10 times and Cyprien R.P. Dube was patted on the shoulder by the Mayor 10 times.

Through it all the terns fished for their nestlings, the flags flew in pure Edwardian tradition, and the band played on. Then it rained and 400 people tried to get into the bandstand along with the band. After a couple of attempts at filming in the deluge, 350 extras were dismissed, saving Universal half a day's pay: an instant savings of $3500.

The 50 remaining extras mugged or watched in the next scene in which – Author! Author! - Peter Benchley (of all people) played the part of a television newscaster and did it darn well, delighting all the directors. He was fully clothed (street clothes, that is, as opposed to the bathing suited bunch) and kept wishing he could take a swim.

Mrs. Benchley and their two children were installed on their blanket as extras, and it was noted that she (like all proper Nantucketers) carried a lightship basket as a handbag, but hers had a shark on top instead of the more orthodox whale.

There is a story, completely untrue, that when Peter Benchley went to California to help write the screenplay, he was not happy with the changes which were being made to his novel. Therefore, to keep peace in the home, the family was cautioned not to mention *Jaws* until one morning everyone appeared wearing a *Jaws* shirt and Peter couldn't help but laugh. *Jaws* was out of Coventry.

Jaws shirts were becoming quite a fad around the set and the Island. They were the usual tourist-type skivvy with *Jaws* spelled out across the back while underneath were lots of teeth surrounded by a maw, a pug nose, a pair of pink eyes and pectoral fins. The shirts weren't worn by everyone on the Island, but it sometimes seemed so.

The table-seated lunch was still served by the side of the road and was now a normal sight to most Islanders. However, to new arrivals in heavily laden station wagons just off the ferry, the site of 160 people sitting at tables eating lunch was not to be believed and traffic came to an open-mouthed standstill.

After lunch more rain fell and the light went dullsville, so the remaining extras, who never knew what was contemplated, were treated to a clarinet concert emanating from the bandstand and the lips of Steve Spielberg. Apparently, he was waiting for someone else to make up his mind.

Someone did make up its collective mind and the male extras were collected and the whole shooting match descended on the Norton and Easterbrooks wharf, in no way increasing the efficiency of the boat yard getting boats overboard for the opening of the racing season the next day.

The man running the dock said, "No, you can't usurp this place now," so someone in the production office called Bill Gilmore, who was in New York, who called Bob Carroll in Edgartown who said, "sure, use the dock." At this point in the *Jaws* endurance test, both the Kelley House and Norton and Easterbrooks boat yard had been saved from financial disaster through the courtesy of *Jaws,* and Bob reasoned, "turnabout is fair play."

Probably due to the fact that Production (out of extreme loyalty) was still getting its weather reports from the National Weather Bureau in Los Angeles (or Baghdad-for-real), shooting for the next day, a Saturday, was called off and scheduled (with time and a half for overtime) on Sunday. But one doesn't outfox Mother Nature easily, so Saturday it was lovely and Sunday it rained.

The 400 who gathered together on the soggy beach spent a damp Sunday morning contemplating a production which was contemplating Hari Kari.

Production dismissed the extras after half a day and told him to come back Monday. But the Islanders knew better. They had been sitting on that beach in the teeth of a northeast wind in what was the first of a three-day northeaster. They also looked at the wind beginning to whip Nantucket Sound and wondered if Production knew the Garage Sale, with the shark platform underneath, was exposed to the brunt of the coming ga;e and on a lee shore to boot.

Production didn't know, since it was now using a forecaster who Barbara Bass said was a hundred percent wrong all summer. Captain Roy Campbell of White Foot suggested moving the rig and the barge but no - Production didn't see anything wrong with where they were.

The storm had its way, as storms will, and S. S. Garage Sale, right in the wind's way, spent a wild night. The guard on board was convinced that he was going to end in a splintered mass on Harthaven beach as waves and water dashed over the barge and through the plastic walls.

White Foot stood by in Vineyard Haven waiting for a call for help, but it didn't come until 4:30 the next day, so by the time Garage Sale was towed into Edgartown everything, including the equipment for operating the sharks, had been well salted down.

The Yacht Club's hoist on the Coal Wharf was used to offload the heavy stuff, but some of the compressed air equipment was too heavy and broke the hoist. Thereafter, there was an unmentionable contretemps between EYC and *JAWS* which never did get settled and the club functioned all summer with a hoist which refused to function.

Wednesday, the third day of the storm, Production put notices up on its door reading, "The weather for the future looks just as bad and therefore extras need no longer check in each night to see if they are on call." This time, Production was right.

During the weather wait the makeup men contended with the problem of the arm. This was left over from the first day of shooting and belonged to Chrissie for fake and Andrea Morton, waitress at the Kelley House, for real. It was supposed to be part of Chrissie's "remains" which washed up on the beach after she had been sharked.

Del Armstrong had made it up and it'd stood on its elbow beautifully posed in the sand and the fact that it was shaking with cold could not be seen. But when the dailies came back, the arm was disappointing. Instead of looking dead and used up, it looked like one of Winged Victory's castoffs. It was pure marble.

So, at the first appearance of good weather the scene was tried again and this time the arm was given a good soaking in a bucket and the unused portions - head, trunk, legs, other arm, etc.- were buried in the sand. The arm was liberally sprinkled with sand, seaweed, and crabs, but it was so cold and had goose pimples running over it, while the crabs refused to move at all. Innovation is the enticement to the movie world and innovation was needed like mad. It arrived in the form of hot coffee, which was poured on the crabs to get them moving, which it did and what the coffee did to the arm was of no concern to *Jaws*.

While *Jaws* was weathered in and contending with arms, the Edgartown Yacht Club opened, people arrived, and the weather finished what it had in mind.

The next time the 400 came back to Baghdad-on-the-Bay to play Fourth of July Beach the last day of June had come, and it looked as if the Fourth would be filmed on the Fourth after all.

It was also apparent that the season was on, and *Jaws* was still in town..

THE SEASON'S ON

There it was - the worst had happened. The summer season was in full swing, and *Jaws* was still in town. The beach scenes were barely started, with their accompanying retakes after the dailies and come back for processing, and the sea scenes with the sharks not yet begun.

Directors were keeping track of where they were in the script by who had been eaten: "Chrissie, the baby boy, the man and the dog."

The weather was warmer and felt like Christmas back in Los Angeles, so the Californians celebrated with a Christmas party complete with lights, tree and action. There were girls in long dresses, red and green ribbons, good food and carols, but it didn't work... Something was missing.

The narrow streets had filled with wandering people just looking; cars looking for parking places and bikes looking for openings in the traffic to dart through, while the harbors filled with cruising boats, speeding boats and lackadaisical sailing boats.

The problems of congestion in the packed town hit the *Jaws* crew hard. Real estate agents were busy finding them new places to stay as their inn rooms were taken by those who had reserved earlier and the houses went the same way.

1974 was a boom summer on the Island regardless of *Jaws*, but the *Jaws* people made it harder because they would never commit themselves for more than a week or two at a time, keep the agents perpetually rewriting leases.

Some of the more expensive houses, which had been put on the market late, might never have rented except for *Jaws*, but the smaller places were in demand regardless. It was that kind of summer.

The agents would be amazed at how readily the Californians would rent a house and think nothing of the $8000 or $12,000 price tag and then complain about the $25 for garbage removal. It was not the summer rents which got them - that been anticipated - but it was the cost of food which they found staggering, mainly because they were used to going to the McDonald's type of restaurants and for this reason many moved into houses in order to cook for themselves only to find food was just as expensive.

Many were pleasantly pleased by the taste of meat and chicken, which they said was much better than California, however they were shocked by the lousy vegetables when they first arrived, not realizing that they as well had been shipped from the coast.

Not only did the Islanders make what Universal spent, but they made from the pockets of those working for Universal. The wife of a sound man spent more than $1000 on antibiotics, and Richard Zanuck's wife spent, "money like water at the drugstore," said Pete Vincent. And all the Californians had to buy new wardrobes or warm clothes.

Then there were the startling amounts spent by Universal on petty unexpected things, and is one salesgirl put it, "what *Jaws* bought they bought in abundance."

There was the standing order for $35 worth of newspapers every day, six days a week, to be used on the Orca; the $118 worth of perfume for a dressing table in the Zinn house and $175 for 5 gallons of glycerin to make the shark's eyes shiny.

New Englanders thought the Californians extravagant, even when they bought for themselves. They were not used to the wild spending and made the most of it while it lasted.

Then too there were the Islanders themselves, who suddenly made money they didn't expect and in an easy-come, easy-go attitude promptly spent it. Lynn Murphy bought a $145 camera and daily batches of Polaroid film for it, as if it were being eaten by the sharks, all three of them.

It was at the start of the season that Universal began paying the rents for some of the principals; an unheard-of occurrence.

This worried Tiggie Woodland of the Carroll and Vincent Real Estate Agency. He had heard that if the studio paid rents the tenants wouldn't give a damn since they were not responsible. "But we were lucky," he said. "The houses were dirty and they were left as if the occupants expected to come right back, with the windows and doors wide open, but there was little damage."

Perhaps this was because many of the Californians were in awe of Edgartown. Here were all of these great big white houses left empty for nine months of the year. Many of the crew owned two or more houses, they worked hard for what they owned and couldn't afford not to have houses that weren't earning their keep. None of them had ever been that close to so much wealth, except perhaps in the movies, and they couldn't believe it.

They weren't quite sure what was an antique and what wasn't, but they took good care of everything just on the chance. Bill Gilmore rented one of the old houses on the south side of town and he and his wife, Paula, were in a panic until they found out that the mirror their children had broken was not in old one.

Living in a pretty old town with a past (which Californians didn't have) they became so interested that when the movie was finished many of them toward the East, visiting Williamsburg, the Freedom Trail and other history preserving sites.

Along with the summer crowds came the annual influx of teenagers looking for summer jobs. Jean Protzman tagged along with a friend who was looking for a job. The friend didn't find one, but Jean did as hostess in the Kelley House dining room. Little did she know what she was getting into, but by the end of the summer she figured she sure had learned a lot.

Not that the *Jaws* bunch was in the dining room that much - they were always out for lunch - but when they were there, people knew it. There were also tourists who came to the Kelley House just on the chance they'd see some of the stars.

Some did, many didn't, and there were those who had no idea what they were seeing. Such as the evening Roy Scheider walked in and calmly announced to all, "The boat sank," and departed.

That was mystifying enough but a half hour later in bounced Rick Dreyfuss, full of excess energy, and shouted, "ladies and gentlemen, the boat sank!" and bounced out. "Strange," thought many in the room.

One morning at breakfast Steve Spielberg, Rick Dreyfuss and Roy Scheider, full of gaiety, started clowning and singing and soon they were standing on their chairs for better delivery. The consensus of the diners seemed to be, "damn actors, can't stop acting, even at breakfast," which the waitresses thought was unfair since the men were just full of such good spirits. Yet one wonders if the room had been empty…

Jean will never forget the night Robert Shaw took author Thornton Wilder and his sister to dinner. They were old friends and had a few rounds of drinks before the Teamsters sent over a round. Then Brown and Zanuck and Teddy Grossman, at a nearby table, sent over another round.

When Thornton Wilder and Robert Shaw headed for the men's room, stuntman Teddy thought that was his cue and made a big play in helping them in and out of the room. They didn't need any help, but it was a good act none the less and played to an appreciative gallery.

Verna Fields decided late in the season that everyone in the movie had been so nice to her that she would have a dinner party at the Harborview where she was staying, and she chose popular and proper buffet night. Jean overheard Roy and Rick deciding to shock the stuffy proper people and shock them they did. How it started no one now admits remembering. It was only to be a noisy sort of upheaval, but things got out of hand and someone started throwing food.

The next day Rick and Roy told Jean it was a shame, they felt that had anyone else behaved that badly they would've been thrown out, but "because it was us we got away with it."

On one occasion what Jean took to be a husband-and-wife came into the dining room all dolled up. They had the demeanor of people acting their best, in their best, and spent a long time over dinner seemingly posing. Observant persons reported such scenes often during the spring and summer. Manners were a good deal better and people were "behaving." Jini Poole suddenly became aware of this after she had been casting for several weeks and the word was out. She noticed people were taking longer to speak to her, looking her more in the eye, enunciating more clearly and being more emphatic. She was sure that they were trying to make her remember them.

The Teamsters lived all summer at the Kelley House where they had 50 rooms. They ate all their meals there because both the room and board were paid for plus the fact that they earned $1000 a week which was more than the actors sometimes got. There's a story that when the Teamsters first arrived, they measured all their rooms to make sure each was the same size and no one who shouldn't had one larger than someone who should. Such is the hierarchy of unions.

In the beginning there had been a roaring controversy about where the Teamsters would come from, whether New Bedford or Boston, but Boston - having the bigger union - won. They were a tough bunch with an entire vocabulary of four-letter words, but by the end of summer Jean remarked, "I've never been around such a fine group of people, even the Teamsters." And as if to prove it, they gave away bikes, cars, radios, leftover liquor and awkward-to-carry items when they left.

Just as *Jaws* broke the sound barrier and entered into the summer season, there was an influx of reporters and cameramen swirling through the swelling town on an entirely different mission. July was the fifth anniversary of the unfortunate Kennedy-Kopechne incident on Chappaquiddick, and it seemed that every news and movie organization was climbing around the satellite Island collecting new material on an old subject. Of course, it wasn't long before they tripped over the *Jaws* contingent thereby making *Jaws* one of the best publicized films. Stories about *Jaws* and sharks were carried by every major publication in the country and a few in Europe.

Filming crews over on the Chappaquiddick Dyke gave rise to new rumors that Universal was making a movie on the sly about Kennedy at the Dyke and secretly flying key figures to Hollywood. "Rumors were half the fun of *Jaws*," said Tiggie Woodland. Production was amused too and kept a bulletin board of printed stories which just weren't so.

As Eastern beaches became crowded Doubleday hired an aeroplane to fly over the heavily populated Jersey shore and Long Island dragging a banner behind it. The banner read, "Swimming? Read JAWS first." According to one magazine sunbathers on Fire Island didn't see the banner because a shark had been reported in the water with them and they were otherwise occupied.

With the season came that great summer celebration, the Fourth of July, and, having spent a good deal of time and money concocting a fake Fourth of July parade, *Jaws* survived to live through the real thing. It was the first holiday for many of the company, who took the chance to get off the Island and tour some of New England, but to others it was a working day (time-and- a-half type working day) and Edgartown's real Fourth of July parade was filmed from the bank, the Catholic Church, and the loggia over the cheese shop.

They got lots more parade for a good deal less effort the second time around plus, by this time, the tree limbs were covered in green and the spectator's limbs were bare and brown. The real parade is sure to have more impact, particularly on those unsuspecting persons who suddenly find themselves on the screen.

The crew couldn't believe their eyes. A week before, the streets had been vacant, and the town was drab but here were literally hundreds of people crammed on Main Street. Then came the fireworks.

These are exploded over the harbor where one gets a stereopticon view if it's calm. As usual, a hive of people occupied beaches, docks and boats. But the Californians, ever conscious of applause, were most impressed by the boat horns which blasted approval at each grand burst. "It's amazing," they said over and over, "we have never heard such appreciation." (They didn't know what fun it is to blow your horn).

BACK TO BAGDAD

The weather didn't settle down to something *Jaws* could use for nearly a week after the first beach scenes had been shot.

Through the lifting morning fog, the flags atop the striped and peaked cabanas were reminiscent of King Arthur's Court on the move. The captains and their merry crews were lucky; they went into the water in wetsuits. That is all but Andy Stone, who seemed to be made of sterner skin than the 400 extras who spent the day alternately getting sunburned on the beach and frozen in the water courtesy of Universal Studios.

All this wetness occurred on Sunday, with time and a half for overtime, when the crew of *Jaws* celebrated the return of more normal weather by filming a mob scene off the Edgartown-Oak Bluffs Road at simulated Baghdad-on-the-Bay.

The band played and sunbathers sunned but only after they were requested to remove their protective warm outer layers and then only for quick rolls of the camera. It was pretty hard to take off that layer of wool and expose quantities of virgin white flesh to the elements (one didn't remember having that much flesh last summer).

It was cold, cold, cold and what sunshine there was proved inefficient for the job. The last day of June was still too early for this sort of thing and not really ideal for spending (all of it - every last bit) on the beach. The leftover northeast winds were still on shore, along with about 600 people.

When Cyprien Dube's make-believe family took their rubber mattress in hand and struck out for Cape Pogue, sympathy mounted as time and again they bravely strode into the cold water pretending it was hot. But sympathy for the Dubes was not enough for Universal; the directors wanted empathy so into the water shivered the 400.

Andy Stone use tact: "Up to now you have had a nice day just sitting on the beach and being paid but now Universal wants you to do something in return. Now you are to be actors. You are to go in the water" -groans- "and panic. I want you to pretend there's a shark in there with you, chasing you! You are being chased by a shark! There's blood in the water!"

The 400 waded out into waist high water (which seemed to be waist high regardless of whether the tide was high or low) and, accompanied by the most outlandish moans, hoots and groans, sank slowly (ever so slowly) to their knees; thus pretending they were up to their necks in water (definitely not hot water) only to be chased right back up on the beach by an imaginary shark.

"We'll go again," said Tom Joyner, and into the Valley of Death waded the 400, with cameras to the right of them and cameras to the left of them.

This did not happen once, or twice, but every five minutes with a regularity becoming only to trans-Atlantic shipping.

"Starting places please," came Tom's amplified voice – groans - "now sink down, the water is deep" - louder groans - "panic-there's a shark in the water! Background action." Off splash the 400 in a real panicky life-and-death swim for shore and the somewhat warmer beach.

By the end of the day the 400 were convulsed with shivers and covered with sand.

One more shot was needed, so the extras were bribed with brandy but Janice Hull shook so much that she spilled all of hers and was told, "it's all right Janice, you don't have to go back in."

"It's a damn damp way to spend a Sunday," thought the Girl Photographer.

Monday came with more of the same but, understandably, with fewer people. Several extras had had it. There was a limit to being a good sport; many had been so cold when they got home the previous night that even after hot baths they were still chattering and most went right to bed to get warm. Plus, the thought of getting into that still damp and sandy bathing suit at six the next morning - just to do it all over again for a mere $20 - seemed to be stretching a point.

Once again it was into the water up to the neck and a wild panic for shore, and as the people crushed shoreward boats beyond the shark net interlaced their wakes, rifles at the ready, while a helicopter skimmed heads.

Everything was repeated for each change of lens and each camera position, the cameras being nearly as athletic as the people. These went up in the helicopter, across the Inlet, down in the sand and out in the water - on a boat or without.

Progress was held up by a little girl in a yellow bikini. She was cute as a button, but a cold button. When asked to duck down, she couldn't do it and stood there shivering with her arms wrapped around her goose pimples.

"Will everyone get down in the water?" tactfully repeated Tom.
Shiver.
""Will the girl in the yellow bikini please get down?"
Continued shivering.
"Get down!" yelled the congealing extras.
"Will the girl in the yellow bikini PLEASE GET DOWN!" begged Tom.

This could have continued forever had not an extra reached up and pulled her down.

Murder was definitely contemplated on another occasion when Peter Benchley was sported laughing his head off as the 400 groaned down to their knees in the getting-colder-each-time water.

One man was supposed to catch his finger in the top of a girl's bathing suit as the 400 raced from the shark, and it was rigged to come off. An overly alert 10-year-old was so intrigued that he never stopped watching the girl and when the top came off he stood up, his eyes as big as Frisbees. The water was supposed to be over his head, so back into the water went the 400.

Everyone put on warm clothes between takes but, regardless, their skin was turning an alarming pink while the surface of the water had taken on a slick of Coppertone and baby oil which certainly must've confounded the Woods Hole Oceanographic Institution when it reached their shore.

One man lost a pair of prescription sunglasses during one take, and found them during another - 800 stampeding feet later.

Another man dashed shoreward clutching half a jagged beer bottle which he had found under those 800 feet, and a woman found something else sharp (the hard way) by stepping on it and had seven stitches taken in her foot. According to Nurse Helen Jackson, it was the first day of her two-week vacation.

By Tuesday, the crowd on the beach had reached huge proportions but only half had been hired, posing another problem since some of them expected to get paid, even after Andy Stone had made countless announcements that persons without cards would not be paid.

As each real extra arrived on any set, his name was checked off Shari's list and he was handed two dollars for lunch (more union rules) and a timecard which was turned in when the extra was dismissed. If he left before dismissal, he did not get paid. But the beach continued to swell with the uninitiated and the uninvited and naturally the directors, always looking for a new face, chose some of the outsiders for special performances.

Such was Dwight Francis, summer-comer West Chop, who came to watch and was given the unusual job of falling on his face in the tide to be trampled on by an onrush of feet. After a morning of this he was asked if he didn't feel a bit trot upon, but he replied through seeping saltwater that he enjoyed it.

Elizabeth (Libby) Warner, always watching everything, was asked to collapse on the beach with a need for artificial respiration.

She lay in the tide, a sandy mess, while her resuscitator bowed and introduced himself as A. James Polk, Jr. of Harthaven.

"Shouldn't you be face down for this?" he asked.

"I should think so," she replied, flipping over on her stomach. "And so we did it the old-fashioned way," she said later. "After all, we were of the pre-mouth-to-mouth age."

After their big scene she and Jim couldn't wait to introduce each other to their respective spouses, only to discover they had already met and had been chatting over the performance.

Jini Poole was supposed to limp out of the water clutching her 12-year-old daughter, Katherine. They did it twice and then Katherine said, "that's too scary," and ran off to play another game.

Devoid of her "prop" Jini limped instead into the hands of a lifeguard and was helped from the water when her leg gave out and she collapsed in the sand. It was during one take that Carol Fligor ambled up and asked if she was all right or should she call a doctor and that scene had to be reshot.

Roy Scheider, acting as police chief Brody, leaned over one of the supposed beach casualties and asked, "Are you all right?" and received a reply, "yes thank you, Roy," and that scene had to be reshot.

Outside the cordon of shark guard boats, Sailfish started by and a chrome plated glass cabin cruiser cruised into spectate, so when a beach ball escaped to open water an ultra-dressy woman on board decided it was a souvenir worth retrieving and reached for it with a desperation which carried her overboard.

Commodore and Mrs. James A. Farrell, Jr. steamed for Edgartown for the first time aboard their new boat – the Koala - and on the way passed the set. The cabanas, with their pitched roofs, were a fair double for those of the beach club on Chappaquiddick point.

As the Koala cruised by, well offshore, Mrs. Farrell looked up from her book and became aware of what seemed to be the Chappy cabanas floating by on the starboard side. Dashing up to the bridge she explained there was shoal water - in fact a whole island - dead ahead.

"But it turned out," she told her friends, "that the captain was navigating by the buoys, not the cabanas," and eventually the Chappy Beach Club showed up ahead just as the buoys and the captain said they would.

As usual there were those who wandered on the set and, thinking it was for real, attempted to buy something, as at the music store.

Nurse Helen Jackson was amazed at the number of people who tried to get something to eat at the fake hot dog stand.

"Just look at this mess," she said to the Girl Photographer, "would you want to eat anything they came out of there?"

Apparently there were those who did, such as the man Helen noticed loitering with intent around the display of cakes on the counter. Finally, he thought he saw his moment and did his shoplifting. Helen delightedly awaited his reaction when he discovered it was fake cake. When it happened, the cake took immediate flight for the trash bin.

Frank Murray, the actor from Falmouth, played the part of a bookseller making the most of the shark scare by selling books about sharks and shark teeth. He eventually became known as the shark boy by the extras who noticed he never stopped pretending to sell books to strangers and extras alike as they wandered about the set. On one occasion he got so carried away that he did sell a book and some teeth before Properties caught up with him.

Helen Jackson was not always watching the loiterers. She always had to be on every set, in case something happened, and most of the time on Fourth of July Beach it did. She was forever extracting bits of shell and glass from bare feet and coping with the never-ending problem of sunburn.

During several of the beach days (not all of them, because it was expensive) a yellow bubble of a helicopter floated about, often huddling behind the cabanas are dashing off on errands known only to the pilot.

Through all this, the band played on, but it become agonizingly apparent that the band knew only one tune. Occasionally some of the players would branch off on their own and attempt something new, but never successfully.

Robert Riger came with his long lens and took pictures for a trade magazine which later had a centerfold of the 400 in full panic. Here again he noted that the first take was the best. He knew it could not be improved upon and to his practiced eye every scene deteriorated with each take, just as at Menemsha. However, he felt the finished product might be one of the best movies ever made and Brown and Zanuck had bitten off the hardest type of special effects. "After all, you can always dress someone up in an ape suit," he told Tiggie Woodland, "but sharks - no wonder they're having trouble."

When his story was published, Universal was so enthusiastic it bought up nearly the whole issue, leaving done for anyone else. Bob Riger also noted that production had been over saddled by the unions of New York and Boston, raising the costs and confusion. In the expensive-expansive line, there was Jack Priestly, a director of photography sent out from New York. He did nothing all summer but pine to get back to work, because Bill Butler was the real director of photography from California and Jack was just a feather in the union's bed.

Whether the site was picked for the script or the script written for the site is not known, but they went together like the chicken and the egg. While the script had the 400 running from the shark (which turns out to be a fake) the real shark slips through an opening into Sengekontacket Pond.

Elizabeth (Libby) Warner was one of the lucky ones who, with her daughter Elizabeth (Betta) was asked to sit on the beach as the shark slipped by. In the pond, Teddy Grossman was to tangle with the shark and those on the beach were to wake up, look up and stand up in horror. But when they watched Teddy do his stuff, as he was being bitten in half by the shark they were so horrified they froze.

Elizabeth (Libby) said later that to the Hollywood people who expected the scene it was an illusion and needed acting to make it look horrible. But to average people like herself, who didn't know what to expect, it was horrible!

Everett (young) had by now gotten wise to the way *Jaws* operated and had rented a Sailfish (the original surfboard with ambition) for $15 a day and had his sister sail it in the movie for $50.

"Put the boat here," Elizabeth (Betta) was told. "Now keep it there... That's fine... but don't let the sail flap."

Betta would stop the sail from flapping which filled it and the boat would sail off.

"No, no, stay where you are," directed the electronic voice. "Now Betta, go back to where we put you," and Betta would appear to be sailing to Europe as she worked her way back up windward where she had started.

"Betta, can you hear me - go back to where you started... there, that's right... now don't move - that's fine, but don't let that sail flap." Betta would trim the sail and off would sail the boat so they would go through it all again.

When Steve realized this wasn't working, he tried it another way. "Now just sail over to that point, Betta - that's fine, but just shove the sail over to the other side of the boat... No! Don't turn the boat around, just put the sail on the other side."

"Huh?" thought Betta on her boat and "Huh?" thought Libby on the beach.

The directors didn't understand sail and to Betta, trying to comply but unable to explain how a sailboat works, this was exasperating. To sailors on the shore, it was hysterically funny.

At this rate $50 a day was turning into a fortune.

A good week and a half were needed to film the scenes around the pond. Either the tide was too high, and the sea sled shark was too deep in the water or the tide was too low and the sled showed. Once again, they had picked a pretty bad spot to work in and many of the scenes done in the pond were redone later.

With no more extras to hire, Shari Rhodes returned to Texas. "It's always so sad," she told Barbara Nevin, "one minute I'm working hard, living deep in the production and then when it is all over I feel lost."

"I know," said Barbara. "I'm dreading it. Like you, I've been so wrapped up with all of this it will be awfully lonely when you all leave. I think I'll keep busy by writing a book about all of you and the making of this movie."

Like an echo from a grave the cabanas remained on the beach for weeks. They were used as background for some fashion models from Saks Fifth Avenue, and by picnickers showing their house guests where it had happened. Then they were used for retakes and left standing in case someone had a bright idea and they might be needed again. They became faded, fell apart a bit, and looked sadder and sadder until they were dismantled and returned from whence they had come - the Fuller Street shed.

SEA CITY

After the beach scenes, Robert Shaw reluctantly returned from his Canadian retreat into the realm of the IRS, and the strange fleet took off for the horizon. Because the director of photography wanted it that way, they used the location off East Chop right in the tide way. Bill Butler couldn't have picked a place with more current, more chop or more boats in the background. Roy Campbell of White Foot told this to Bill and a few others but, as he noted again, "they just don't listen."

Since the beginning of the industry, the camera has been placed, the actor placed, lights positioned, distance measured, and cameras focused. And since the beginning of time boats have followed the line of least resistance and swung with the wind, tide or sometimes both. Therefore, every boat, raft, rubber mattress or Sailfish used in the production had to be anchored at all four corners; held rigid against wind and tide. It was a situation rather like the irresistible force and the immovable object.

Scenes would be set up ready to go when a new current slightly shifted the boats. They would then have to be re-anchored and by the time this had been accomplished the sun would've moved.

The shooting flotilla consisted of about 16 boats. The tugboat, White Foot, served as mothership, restaurant, base, "john" and tow boat. The old City of Chappaquiddick was still the electric barge, and as such her flush deck carried lights, camera and action. She was a jumble of equipment; clothing, lenses, filters, arc lights, cables and potato chips. As many as 65 people climbed over the paraphernalia, slipped between it or fell into its cavities. Herschel West and his poodle, Tipper, acted as helmsman and one of them (no one is sure which) kept the constant cachet of cookies and Coke stashed somewhere in the bowels of this bedlam

A pile-driver was the generator barge and carried what wouldn't fit on the electric barge, including her own supply of plastic cups and potato chips. The star of the flotilla was the Orca (later there would be an Orca II), the only one to get her picture "took"- supposedly alone upon the vacant sea.

There was the S. S. Garage Sale, that great hulk towering into the skyline with the ridiculous shark spinning atop the roof gable. She was the control center for special-effects and the sharks. There were also the dry-docks for the sharks not in use, and Lynn Murphy's Valerie N. with winches for towing the sled shark and a compressor for activating it.

These floating curiosities were attended by a fleet of outboards and inboards, controlled by walkie-talkies. There often repeated names were Popeye, Got-cha, Fascinating Rhythm, Ruddyduck, Itchy, Flossy, Whaler and Jaws. For special-effects dirty work there was an ever-increasing fleet of rubber Zodiacs and rowboats.

The smaller boats were the taxis, continually dispatched on errands; ashore for garbage bags, to sea with the coffee, back for some more potato chips, in for the director, out with a visitor, in for lumber or out for scattered sundries. They hummed like bees around the flotilla when not on trips ashore so that they could be hailed by crew members wishing to transfer to another boat.

Twice a day the big coffee urn would go out, with coffee and cocoa in the mornings and coffee and soup in the afternoons. There were 10 of them labeled Garage Sale, Electric Barge or wherever they were destined.

Along with the morning coffee went the doughnuts and coffee cake until Rick Dreyfuss got the idea of bagels and cream cheese - and that, ladies and gentlemen, is what happened to Rick's waistline. There was also the problem of peanut butter, which got so acute that it was not allowed to be mentioned. Salt air is famous for increasing the appetite so quantities of peanut butter and crackers were purchased by glib souls who would saunter into the Edgartown Market, pick up munchables and call out, "charge it to Universal."

The experiences encountered on the high seas are not to be believed. Robert Shaw continued to get seasick but that was no longer a problem. Everything was hard. No one out there really knew about water, wind, tide and sunburn. Takes took forever to set up and everyone not working went out of his mind with boredom (the clever ones went to sleep). Robert Shaw, in a television interview, said that it wasn't long before he, Rick and Roy knew every intimate detail of each other's lives, their parent's lives and their own sex lives.

Platforms and stages - detachable, raiseable, floatable and otherwise - were used on all the big boats, including the Orca, for cameras to the right, cameras to the left, cameras over the water, on the water or in the water.

Many was the time that all 60 people would crowd aboard the 42-foot Orca which was rafted to other craft so that lights could shine directly into the cabin windows or into the cockpit. This work in the tideway was dangerous, and although there were those who went overboard, no one was hurt.

Not only were the boats hard to handle, but the sharks were impossible. They had been tested to the extent that they wore out and yet, when Bob Mattey and Stan Mahoney operated them, sharks often popped up in the most unexpected places.

To make all of this insanity (and it was insanity - there is no doubt about that) easier, Joe Alves drew pictures like funny papers for each of the sea scenes in the third act. This meant that the different episodes could be shot from the same location at one time, out of sequence - all the shooting from the crow's nest or all the shooting from the water level - but for some reason it didn't work that way and many of the scenes were shot in almost consecutive order.

Filming was done from the shark's eye view. Day or night, from the distance, from the cabin looking out, looking in, looking down on the Orca from the rigging, looking up at her from the water, looking aft from the bow, looking forward from the aft while the three men aboard – Roy, Rick and Robert - were pictured in the normal circumstances of eating, storytelling or the wild confusion of fighting one another - or the shark, which eventually came aboard to join the fray.

Other problems were the curious strangers sailing into Edgartown who saw this aberration on the skyline and naturally sailed over to investigate. Of course they wouldn't know what they were looking at, and lingered to figure it out until one of the smaller craft steamed over to ask them to leave. The little boats often sped into the empty seas to ask one lone sailor to "please get the hell and gone out of the background."

With hardly any variance, *Jaws* continued to work in what Production called "Cow Bay," which was really Nantucket Sound and offered none of the protection the word "Bay" denotes. They worked either under East Chop or Cape Pogue, depending on which way the wind was blowing, but this is just where the Edgartown Yacht Club held its "around the bouys" race. Then, to top it off, there was the Edgartown Yacht Club Regatta and the arrival of the New York Yacht Club squadron. Plus, this was an America's Cup year to boost. These are possibly the best sailing waters in the world, and here was *Jaws* right in the middle and requesting solitude.

Someone finally convinced Bill Butler that "Cow Bay" wasn't the place to work and he then tried the backside of Cape Pogue, right in the tides and shoals of Muskeget Channel and was confronted by fishing boats splashing to and from the rips which cluttered up the background and rocked the boats with their wakes.

Roy Campbell suggested Katama Bay for the third or fourth time, but the conglomerate of madmen wasn't for it.

While this desperate disaster clustered upon the skyline, Barbara Bass found herself still stationed on the Norton and Easterbrooks dock for three months. Here she controlled what when seaward in the way of small boats, gear, lumber, food, and passengers.

The narrow street which ran down to the dock was cramped with trucks on hand to produce supplies at the drop of a shark's tooth, and in the yard's tiny parking space the commissary truck sat with its attendant tables. These were constantly filled with the Teamsters playing cards or cribbage and a sound man repairing (or trying to repair) the walkie-talkies which went overboard.

Jaws used Motorola two-channel walkie-talkies which cost about $1000 each, so when there was a rash of them going overboard orders went out that they would have to be tied to the operator. Sensible thinking - all sailors learn to use lanyards attached to their belts on anything they are fond of which doesn't float - knives, marlinspikes, fids and themselves, while binoculars and cameras are always hung around the neck - never from a shoulder.

The only trouble was that Production, in its consistently un-nautical way, lashed only the holster to the belts, so that the instruments themselves when held to the mouth became as free as a Kingfisher and made the same splash as they hit the water.

In the early stages everyone was brought ashore for lunch, but with 65 people traveling in small boats this took forever. As the set became a city at sea it was easier to take lunch out to White Foot where a table was set up and the ever-present Helen Jackson would help serve lunch. While the Teamsters sat down to those famous tables for lunch on the wharf, the stars and the directors sat on bollards or coils of line and ate from trays.

Rolly Harper's Catering Service did the cooking and it was the best. Six days a week, good food consistently came out of that galley, ordered and cooked by two men who usually fed about 160 people. They ordered the food for each meal two weeks in advance from the mainland, then started work with their baking at 4:30 in the morning. There were always two choices of meat, potatoes, vegetables, salad, dessert, milk, chocolate milk, coffee and boxes of apples and oranges, the like of which most New Englanders never see.

It can only be supposed that many who shouldn't ate that lunch. On one -or maybe more - occasions someone yelled, "Lunch is ready," so a cleaning woman (who had no connection with *Jaws*) sat down with her two children. Universal paid the bill, which was tallied by the cooks who counted the used trays.

For the people who lived on North Water Street it was a different summer. Mrs. Francis F. Randolph had her parking lot usurped by the Teamsters who moved in their tables for cards. She didn't and parked on the street. She liked the Teamsters and they liked her.

Mr. and Mrs. E. Jared Bliss lived on the other side. Mrs. Bliss didn't sleep well and the generators, which roared into action at 6 a.m., didn't help. The Teamsters' language also didn't help - it wasn't the best - and the congestion on the dock didn't help much either but the Bliss's had a front row seat on the excitement and entertained wives of crew members.

The many wheels on the double-barreled honey wagon were beginning to rust in the salt air and it was so large that it had to back up a whole block to get off the dock each night on its way to the sewer plant where it was emptied. An owner of a red truck used to pump out the local cesspools, couldn't resist and painted "Amity Re-used Water Company" on the rear of his truck.

While *Jaws* functioned on the front and back ends of the wharf the normal services of a boat yard were carried on around the edges as the yard's launch, Nor'East, landed yachtsmen into the melee. She still wore the red sign saying "Harbor Patrol" - left over from the beach scenes - which must've confused many of the passengers into thinking they were being arrested instead of taxied.

While the dock reigned supreme as the jumping off place for the city on the sea, another drama was progressing in the Fuller Street boat shed and the selectmen were again receiving complaints.

SINKING ORCA AND A STOLEN SHARK

Back at the Fuller Street boat shed where the sets had been made, crews were working day and night in a continual race against time. Cars and trucks came and went at all hours, lights flared, and machines chugged. Neighbors complained, it was not only spooky, but it was keeping them awake.

One of the neighbors was the still photographer, Lewis Goldman, who was so tired after his daily stint at sea nothing could keep him awake but there were others, and they went to the selectmen and complained that enough was enough. They had put up with the building of cabanas and gazebos, the secret storage of sharks, the cluttering of the yard with the restrooms from Fourth-of-July beach, the walls from the Menemsha house, sharks wagging their tails from the loft and now it was hammers and sawing and acetylene torches all through the night.

The citizens and the selectmen pronounced judgment on Production and said, "Shut down by 11:30 so residents can sleep." This was agreed, but the work still had to go on.

Among the creations in the shed was a duplicate of the Orca. When the first one had been finished she had been used as a plug to fiberglass a duplicate.

Boats since the beginning of time have been built to float, or at least that's the object, but Universal Studios (which had been doing the unusual right along) was building a boat to sink. The idea sounded a bit odd, and the boat, when she appeared, looked a bit odd. The Orca was Quint the shark killer's boat and the Orca II was to be sunk by the shark.

After the second Orca was cast, the bottom of the hull beneath the water line was cut off and replaced by a steel scaffolding welded to her topsides. In the rack formed by the scaffold were rows of barrels, which could be filled either with compressed air or water depending on whether the Orca was to be sunk or unsunk.

Naturally, the directors were not going to do anything once - that wasn't their style – and therefore the boat was going to have to go up and down about as often and with as much dexterity as a seagull opening a stubborn clam. Since the Island doesn't have a Stevens Institute tank for testing, and undoubtedly there are no records of tank testing of this sort, all was hypothetical until they could get her finished and in the water.

The new Orca was too tall for the shed, so she had to be built in split levels. Four extra transoms were built, one of pine - which was the real stern - and the three others of balsa for the sharks to splinter. There were also extra engine hatches of balsa, so one got the idea of what was going to happen to the poor boat.

Regardless of her future, she was perfect down to the last detail, even to the control panels in the wheelhouse and on the flying bridge which had real instruments (their wires hanging): tachometers, depth finders, compasses, gear shifts, wheels, and light switches. Even the cabin soles were constructed with the same skill and care as the real Orca including lovely little louvered shutters.

Although the work in the shed was carried on in desperation it was hampered by the fact that the Orca II was being built on an Island. Island welders weren't up to this creativity, so Production had to bring its own from California. Production, used to demanding what it wanted and getting it within an hour later, had to import materials.

It was to be the middle of August before she was finished, painted, then painted with dirt and rust to match her predecessor and trundled down to the hoist at the yard.

While the sinking Orca was being constructed in the shed, the real Orca sank. This happened, at the end of the day's shooting just as they were about to wrap, out in "Cow Bay."

As the 3 R's - Roy, Rick and Robert - were battling the shark, which was trying to board them, and to simulate the effect, the Orca had been firmly anchored by her port eyebolts and two boats were jerking her from the star board. Something on the old boat had to give and it was a port plank.

Tom Joyner was on the radio telling Bill Gilmore in the office that they had finished the scene and were going to wrap, when he noticed his feet were getting wet and offhandedly remarked, "The Orca appears to be sinking." Then he noticed that his knees were wet and, making a reappraisal, yelled,

"THE ORCA IS SINKING!!"

Jonathan Filley, operating one of the launches, had pulled over to the shore and was shooting the breeze with his father when someone bellowed at him, "Hurry up, were sinking."

They were also yelling at Roy Campbell on White Foot to come over and haul them out of the water with his crane, but with no result. White Foot didn't move. The Orca was going down pretty fast and Jonathan Filley had just deposited a load of people from her to another boat when it occurred to him and Charlie Blair that the thing to do was beach her.

Charlie, a blue water sailor, quickly got a line on Orca's bow and headed for shore. He made it to within 15 feet were upon Jonathan, in a little Boston Whaler, gave her a final push and she was beached.

Barbara Bass, back in the boat yard, had been informed that the boats were coming in and went to clear the outboard end of the dock and found an abandoned sailboat, left by a woman who had yelled, "We'll be back for the boat later, my husband's had a heart attack."

Barbara had a strong apprehensive feeling when she saw the boat's name was Amity.

It was not until 10 PM that the Orca was towed in, propped up on the ways and Kenny Dietz was called in to salvage her water-soaked engine. They worked through the night and had her back on station for the shark to tear apart in the morning.

This time the Orca was "supposed" to catch fire after her engine exploded only, in true *Jaws* style, she really did catch fire.

Special effects men had been pouring oil on the hot exhaust, sending up great pillows of smoke. This was fine until they poured on too much. As the smoke from fake, and eventually real, fires piled into the sky, they were spotted by some irritatingly alert young pilot who reported a burning boat to the Coast Guard.

Once again, the Coast Guard gave all concerned a tongue lashing which no one needed, as Barbara said, "In a business where it costs $1000 a minute you can't stop for little things like burning boats."

Near the end of August, the Orca II was still perched on the hoist, just in case. There it was discovered that the scaffold had been improperly assembled and more masters of the acetylene torch were imported.

Joe Alves and Stan Mahoney had been the masterminds of the Orca II along with Robert Mattey so the three of them put in extra hours re-planning and refitting until at last she went up and down on command (they should've called her Otis).

Through the weeks, through the summer crowds and normal activities there sat this strange bottomless craft, normal on top and a jungle gym beneath.

Orca, the honey wagon - with the Universal dressing rooms - the trucks and Teamsters were the only visible evidence of *Jaws* in town during the day. But as the last light turned the harbor waters turquoise blue and the east purple, the strange little fleet, running lights a twinkle, would trail into the harbor carrying their exhausted illusion-makers home.

They'd be off again so early in the morning that most tourists weren't up to see them go. The crews went first, setting up the boats in new positions for the day's shooting. S. S. Garage Sale always remained on station over the platform with other nautical oddments which consisted of "Location." The more agile craft put into Edgartown for the night, while the sharks were taken home to Shark City in Oak Bluffs.

One evening a boat owner, towing a dry dock with the sea-sled shark, arrived at his berth on Oak Bluffs to find that it had been usurped by another craft. He was wild. He was also tired, and what's more if he didn't get tied up and plugged in soon his milk would sour. According to Barbara Bass he grabbed a hatchet and hacked apart the electric cable which plugged in the trespassing tar.

"Hey, you can't go about destroying other people's property," yelled the dock watchmen.

"Yeah," said the boat owner, "well I don't give a good God damn about other people's property. To hell with the bunch of you."

He stormed back to his boat and tore out of the harbor into the fog, forgetting he still had the shark on behind.

The concerned watchman telephoned the Edgartown police that a wild man had been destroying other people's property and, having stolen one of the sharks, was headed for Edgartown.

Into the pea soup steamed the boat and shark while down to the dock went the Edgartown constabulary. There they waited, listening into the fog.

"It's pretty damn thick," thought the boat owner. Let's face it, it WAS thick, and for the life of him he couldn't find the dock, but he was on the right approach when he fetched up on someone's mooring and fouled the pennant around a propeller.

The police, listening in the fog, heard him arrive and then they heard him cuss and then, along with the cussing, they heard splashing as of things being jettisoned.

"Good God! Bits of shark!" thought the constabulary, "now he's chopping up the mechanical shark!" So, they purloined a rowboat.

"God dammit to hell!" and worse bellowed the boat owner entangled in the mooring, and pitched over a collection of anchors to hold him through the night.

Into the fog rowed the constabulary where they homed in on the cursing and arrived at the boat. She was boarded and the boat owner, still swearing, was carted off to jail.

When filming began in the early morning off Cape Pogue, Production was short one shark. "Where the hell is it?" demanded voices in the fog. "Find it!" said all the walkie-talkies to one another.

Universal may not have known where their sea-sled shark was, but some residents of the Edgartown waterfront did. As the sky lightened and the fog lifted there were the two beady eyes of the shark and a row of bottom teeth glaring in their windows. The more the fog lifted the more the denizen loomed.

To protect the shark from prying eyes, lenses and sun it'd been covered with a form-fitting tarpaulin which only made it more appealing as it peaked out from underneath. The harbor front telephones were busy that morning and so was Barbara Bass who drove up to the jail with Tom Joyner to bail out the boat owner. Nevertheless, it was several days and some few tries before the mooring was untangled and the shark was back on location.

Eventually, the Orca II made it into the depths and out again, proving she could sink and un-sink. However, to be on the safe side, shoal water was chosen so she would have something to sit on when she was down.

Roy Campbell was still in the background sounding like a broken record saying, "why don't you work in Katama Bay?" This time they listened. The tug took sinking Orca up the bay where she was retested, sinking to the right or left, with stern up or bow up (she was a very versatile sinker) though getting her at just the right angle was complicated.

While sinking Orca was doing her stuff in Katama Bay the shark was still battering away at the Orca in "Cow Bay." Roy hadn't gotten them all in the real bay yet, but he was working on it.

ALL AT SEA AND A STRIKE

While the shark was knocking hell out of the Orca out in "Cow Bay" and the Orca II was practicing sinking in Katama Bay, the town entered the hectic second phase of summer, all out and gung ho. The middle of August had come, when added to the normal hecticisms, every church and organization has a fund-raising while the money is still around.

The 3 R's - Rick, Roy and Robert - along with Joe Alves, had been asked to give an "Evening with *Jaws*" for the benefit of the Old Sculpin Art Gallery and even a pair of jaws had been borrowed from *Jaws* so that children could have their pictures taken through them at the St. Andrews Fair. Production was good to the town.

On location as the days grow shorter the working hours grew longer and the work harder and more dangerous. The little boats used as launches still scurried between the larger anchored craft or to shore on 1000 errands in what Roy Campbell considered the worst waste of time and fuel he had encountered to date. His staunch New England character was galled.

Drivers of the little boats were paid $90 for a normal working day - 10 hours (no longer in fashion). On top of this 10 hours there was more likely than not more work, so the taxi boatmen formed a union and went on strike.

Production was wild, Bill Gilmore was wild, the Teamsters were wild and filming was held up. Into the little boats went the Teamsters and, trying to help, only made matters worse. Theirs's was the open road, not this splashy stuff, so it wasn't their fault that things went wrong. Trucks could be parked and trusted to stay put, but not boats; the darn things had to be tied up like dogs or they'd wander off on their own. And what do you do with them out on the water when there is nothing to tie them up to?

Production staggered along and refused to sit down to the conference table no matter what shape it was. Then the union threatened to complicate filming by sailing through the background and Production gave in.

The Teamsters were wild, Bill Gilmore was wild, and the special effects men were wilder. Here they were, drawing deep water diving pay, walking around the ice water on the bottom of Nantucket Sound (they still thought it was Cow Bay) risking life and limb and freezing to death while a bunch of little rich at a summer resort were paid more for running their boats on the top of the water.

"Bunch of spoiled kids," seemed to be the customary remark.

On the side of drivers, they were spending long hours out there in a mass of guy wires and rigs resembling Medusa's head, making dangerous maneuvers in a manner new to them. They were used to sanity, not the making of movies, and this headlong do-or-die rush to destruction was not for them.

The do-or-die rush led to hard use and mutilation of equipment, so that Stanton Richards at the Yacht Club couldn't get over the huge sums of money spent to make money. "It seemed to be just waste and fiasco, and says something about the American economy."

Whatever the reason, by the end of the summer owners had a hard time recognizing the boats they rented to *Jaws* because they were pretty beat up and worn-out.

After the taxi-boat strike, location was at last moved to Katama Bay where the water didn't get chewed as much by the wind, where the currents were less strange and less time had to be spent commuting between location and Edgartown.

"They listened," thought Roy Campbell, "I don't believe it."

"They should have been working up there all along," said most of the Islanders. Conditions were perfect.

The part where the shark finally leaps aboard the Orca was filmed and re-filmed with such regularity that one man became accustomed to entertaining his houseguests by taking them out to watch. And what fascinating tales must've been told when they reached civilization, and what unbelievable snapshots they would have to show for the rest of their lives.

During the summer there were so many people out taking pictures of sharks, *Jaws* and the like, that cameras were going overboard right and left or, rather, port and star board so the Girl Photographer received a rash of what-do-I-do-with-it-now calls from owners lucky enough to retrieve them.

There is nothing to do for a drowned camera anymore then for a drowned walkie-talkie but get it dry, rush it to a repair man and pray. But the Girl Photographer didn't tell them this because she was a sissy and advised them to call up *Jaws*. Surely all those fabulous well-paid cameramen would know what to do. That was the easy way out, but when the still photographer's camera went overboard and Louis Goldman asked for help, she couldn't very well send the *Jaws* photographer to do *Jaws* cameramen.

They should have known how to take cameras apart the way they babied their Panavisions and the Panaaflex. Each night these were dried with hairdryers, polished, cleaned, and oiled. During the day, when the cameras were to be near the surface of the water, they went there in a water box with a glass front and all the shooting was dryly done from the inside. The water box for the Panaflex was what made it possible for Dwight Francis to be filmed at eye level, face down in the water and for pictures from the shark's eye point of view.

At the least suspicion that something might splash on the cameras; salt, blood or squid, they were wrapped in plastic bags or bundled in bath towels. During one of the numerous times a boat was thought to be sinking, cameraman Michael Chapman is reputed to have snatched a life jacket off a human and put it on a camera. The big cameras thus receive better care than the people but then, they cost more.

The story is that the Panaflex camera alone cost $2400 a week to rent, and then there were all the filters, sunshades, lenses, controls for zooms, tripods, dollies, sights, viewers, and motors, all transported in their own truck.

The little Panaflex camera was the untried heroine of the film. It was compact enough to handhold; fit in water boxes, be rigged on bowspirits, crow's nests, buried in the sand or sit on laps. Tripods with Gyro heads were often impossible since the boats rocked too much, and handholding the little camera seemed steadier. Thus, this may well be the first widescreen Panavision movie made with a handheld camera. The test will be whether the viewers get seasick or not.

Into the business of filming came Tom Ellis of WBZ-TV. He was here trying to buy a house and conceived the idea of an Island documentary instead. Therefore, he was looking for famous people who would come out of the bushes where they lived to be interviewed, but the Walter Cronkites were the ones he caught and mainly because they were already in the maw of *Jaws*.

The Cronkites were new to the Island, it was only their second summer, but they were so in love with the place that they had bought a house, not up-island in the tangle of scrub oak - where they couldn't be found - but right on a hill overlooking Edgartown Harbor. This was because Mr. Cronkite is a sailor who derives the greatest pleasure from looking out his windows and watching his ketch, Wyntie, spin at her mooring.

Jaws needed Wyntie - it was cooking up something new - and Tom Ellis attacked at the same time, so the Cronkites were hooked before they knew it, thereby wasting a good sailing breeze.

Carl Gottlieb and Steve Spielberg had gotten the bright idea of having a bunch of boats lighted for Fourth of July and while people partied on board in the balmy night, the shark was to thread its way unnoticed between them into the harbor.

It was now the Fourth of July in September and the Charles Blairs' Hot Foot was on her mooring and Wyntie on the dock while special effects men and gaffers rigged them fore and aft with colored Christmas lights which were strong international code fashion up the headstay and down the backstay connected to motorcycle generators.

While Walter Cronkite's beloved boat was being wired up in this unheard-of fashion, Tom Ellis and his crew were wiring him and his family with microphones. Then, as the Chappy ferry plied back and forth, the television cameras rolled, the Cronkites were duly interviewed and the good breeze blew itself out.

Walter Cronkite was embarrassed. "Do people really decorate their boats like this here?" he asked the Girl Photographer.

"No, never," she replied, "they do it in Miami for a New Year's parade, but not here - never!"

"I shouldn't think so, I'm too embarrassed to be on her. People will think I don't know any better," and with this he scooped up his two Mrs. Cronkites (one his mother and one his wife) and went over to the Dickinson's Cruzan, telling Freddie Zendar, "put her back at her mooring when you're finished with her."

Chuck and Fanny Blair, along with their son Charlie, sat on board Hot Foot. "I wonder if they planned it this way?" mused Chuck. "What way?" asked Fanny, eyeing the big shark at the dock.

"The tide, it's just shifted, and is going the right way for what they have in mind. If it hadn't, they'd have to be out here anchoring these boats at all four corners to keep them from swinging the wrong way."

"It's a wonder if they have," said Charlie. He been one of the taxi-boat drivers before the strike and had a whole list of marine mishaps. "These people are so un-nautical that once…" he stopped talking as the shark in its drydock, which had been "tied" to the dock without benefit of hitches, began to move into the channel. Speedily a man jumped into an outboard with the intention of pushing it back to the dock but instead of pushing he pulled.

The shark was attached to a compressor on the dock so that when the shark departed it towed the compressor into the water.

"… See what I mean?" finished Charlie.

After the compressor had been hauled up from the bottom of the channel it needed to be rinsed and hair dried before the shark was put in the water, but the compressor had lost something by taking the plunge and could no longer sustain the shark.

Left to its own devices it did what any real shark would do under the same circumstances and slewed off down-stream where it headed for the bottom. There, it managed to entangle itself in the Chappaquiddick telephone and light cables.

As hundreds waited impatiently, divers were hindered in the rescue operations by the Chappy ferry which continued its back and forth run. This was Sunday evening and departing weekenders had connections to make.

Dick Hewitt finally had to stop the ferry, but not as rumor had it - because the shark's rubber hoses had wrapped around his propeller.

Ironic as it may seem this is the same channel which Sen. Edward Kennedy is reputed to have swum on a July evening, which some Islanders found hard to believe since they know that such a channel, between two islands, is where sharks forage after dark and this selfsame channel is liable to contain a mako or two on a warm summer night.

Obviously, with all this going on, Tom Ellis and his crew could not overlook *Jaws* and they became so fascinated with the operation that they visited the set for the next several days, photographing, recording and interviewing Steven Spielberg and the 3 R's. He got there just under the wire because Robert Shaw was departing to get out of reach of the IRS which was only a day's pounce behind him.

To let him escape, Jini Poole was given 24 hours to find a double. So she trod the public beach at Menemsha. "When a man is sitting down, how do you know what he looks like standing up?" She discovered a likely suspect and he promptly asked her to sit down and tell him all about it, so he could tell his wife. Cute bubbly Jini is not the type to pick anyone up, but he didn't know that and wanted to be safe. Finally, he told her to come back when the price went up. $2.50 an hour wasn't enough.

Eventually someone was found and, with a double and a stuntman to fill in for him in the shark's mouth, Shaw left the country, but two days late so there were extra greenbacks in Uncle Sam's blue jeans.

Overly bouncy Rick Dreyfuss was getting obstreperous so Jini was looking for a double for him as well when one walked right into the production office. He had never heard of Rick so he didn't know that he looked like him and couldn't have been more surprised when everyone on the set agreed. Even Rick himself gave one look and said, "You found my double, start right now, I'm going out to dinner."

One of the grips looked at Jini and said, "You know if you put this in a movie, no one would believe it."

OUT IN A BLAZE OF GORY

By now the production that was to have taken five weeks or 30 shooting days had taken five months or 120 shooting days and, while every day was going to be the last, the climax was still building.

The shark finally made it aboard the Orca and promptly ate Robert Shaw. Normally that would be a once-in-a-lifetime thing, but not in the movies. Robert Shaw was therefore eaten several times.

One reason many in the crew found it hard to work for Steve Spielberg was his intense concentration when creating. He would become so wrapped up in his moment that the mechanics of the scene never penetrated his head. When he wanted the impossible, he got it - it just took forever. While the shark was munching on Teddy Grossman, Steve was calling for more action of the jaws, were thrashing of the shark, more speed, more power but Stan Mahoney, at the controls, realized the action was reaching the danger point. It was hard to control the tons of hydraulic pressure at a rapid pace with a live man in those jaws, so he yelled that something was wrong and the jaws wouldn't work. (For the next shark scene, the jaws worked perfectly which was a little puzzling to some - but not all).

The shark versus Shaw scenes had been so rough and the struggle so intense that the shark lost most of its teeth. Then, while digesting Robert Shaw, it continued to flop about the Orca, inserting itself into the cabin in a surge similar to the wild feeding frenzies of shark packs.

All this while the Orca was sinking to a predetermined position, at just the right angle. Again and again the scene was redone then, on one of the takes, the Orca went too far, thereby dunking one of those precious Panavision cameras and a day's take of film.

Had it been a human who had gone down with the ship, or the camera alone, the situation would not have been too bad but a whole days take was a tragedy. The camera and the film were packed in saltwater and immediately flown to New York by private jet, where the film turned out to be fine. As for the camera, no one bothered to find out, and a replacement was immediately flown East.

Each day Production hoped to be finished, but something else always turned up. Verna Fields, doing her on-the-site editing, would need something; a new angle or an insert, so to save time she directed the second camera crew and, with Barbara Bass, tried to get some footage of the rubber mattress floating ashore devoid of the shark-eaten boy.

What should have been a simple 15 minutes of work lasted 2 ½ hours. There was no wind and no pushing waves. Cameramen, directors and grips tried splashing, shoving, towing and wave creation, but nothing worked. In the end, before the set of the sun, Barbara used a broom and ladled the mattress to shore.

There was also a bunch of retakes from Sengekontacket Pond, which would now be done in Katama Bay, and Production, knowing it would have to call an end before the snows flew, scheduled all the local players to be shot while available and all the scenes connected with the sinking Orca to be finished. She was be left behind along with the S.S. Garage Sale and the drydocks. The real Orca and the sharks were to go back to Hollywood where shooting would continue - and continue it did - until the middle of February.

Matters in those final days would have run more smoothly had it not been for pettiness on the part of officialdom. Universal had a big shark head, the first one that was ever made as a model for the rest. Thinking that it might come in handy it had been shipped East with the rest of the gear. Brown and Zanuck wanted a more spectacular ending then Peter Benchley's, so they plotted to have Roy Scheider - rapidly going down in the Orca's cabin because the shark was blocking the door - jam a cylinder of oxygen in the shark's mouth. This took about 75 takes, but it was finally accomplished. However, the keyed-up shark didn't realize it was hampered in any way and continued to attack. Therefore, it was up to Brody - or Roy Scheider, who didn't know who we was at this point - to fire a rifle at the oxygen and thus blow up the whole works, shark and all.

But Edgartown - town of and selectmen of - were suspicious: dynamite was to be used and this sounded illegal, immoral and fattening. Fire chiefs and fire marshals found nothing wrong with it, and indeed there wasn't. Universal did this sort of thing all the time in Westerns. But harangue ensued. More marshals and under-marshals were called down from Boston for a confab in the town counsel's office, and there were a lot of petty grievances, past and present, to do with *Jaws* -pre-*Jaws* and post *Jaws* -which had to be spun out into legalese. In the end it turned out that Edgartown just had to have a real reason why the shark's head could not be blown up. The reason was not found, and the permit was signed, provided a specialist in demolition from the Woods Hole Oceanographic Institution set the charge.

Jaws was determined to go out in a blaze of gory. The actual shark's head could only be blown up once, that's true, but other explosions from other angles could be simulated.

A dozen gallon tins filled with red paint and squid labeled "blood and guts" were exploded by compressed air between Roy and the camera.

"Lord, this place will be a sea of blood," said Bill Butler, pointing at the crammed deck of the City of Chappaquiddick. "You'd better get some plastic and cover all of this and the camera."

Roy climbed into the crow's nest on the Orca, the rest of which was sitting on the bottom 30 feet down. The rifle went off, the compressed air went off, the "blood and guts" went up and the Girl Photographer went over backwards into the sea of red paint and dead squid. (The red paint came off, eventually, but six cameras smelt of squid for six months thereafter).

As she gathered herself out of the slimy mess, she looked questioningly at Bill Butler, who had been standing next to her when the charge went off and who was still on his feet.

"I was expecting it," he said kindly.

The same scene was shot until nearly sundown when the gaffer surprised everyone by saying, "I've got to oversee the loading of the truck; the lights are leaving for California in the morning."

Rick Dreyfuss and Roy Scheider did the final scene while Steve Spielberg read off the imaginary credit crawl to time it, and it was - finis!

Steve stayed on to do a few of those inevitable unending retakes the next day, and the demolition boat came from Woods Hole to set the charge of dynamite in the shark's head. A special wide angle camera arrived with its 16 lenses and all available cameras were set up along the roof of Garage Sale, when Bill Butler realized that, since the shark's head was up wind (they had learned about such things - finally) the cameras and their merry crews were in for a "blood and guts" soaking, and from the smell of the Girl Photographer this was to be avoided. Lumber was quickly ferried out from shore and the grips built a protecting battlement on the roof.

Before they finished, never-still-a-second Steve Spielberg was off in another boat throwing marbles into the water with Michael Chapman taking pictures as they hit. It seems that marbles make bullets hitting water in movie-ese. Seconds later Steve was involved making leftover shark retakes and Teddy Grossman was back in the shark maw, so the shark's head never did get set off and Steve left for California that night.

There were several more shark retakes done the following day and this time Joe Alves, the art director who heretofore had been a bit critical of the length of time it'd taken to shoot the simplest of scenes, was to have his day in the sun and do the directing.

His first scene was a retake of the Kintner boy being eaten off his rubber mattress. The shark was to make his appearance subtly in the far background while children would be splashing in the foreground. To make the shark even more subtle the camera would be looking into the sun. This scene had originally been done in shoal water, now it was done in 30 feet.

Barbara Bass suddenly thought of those small children out there in 30 feet of water and realized they would need flotation which wouldn't show. Waterskiing belts were the thing, but there were none on the Island. Eventually she tracked down a man who had just bought 30 of them for his boat, and although he refused to sell, he did land.

Experience being the best teacher, Barbara also sent out several relays of children. The water was getting cold again.

Joe Alves arrived early and enthusiastically at S. S. Garage Sale and in no time had the camera set up, but Special Effects was having trouble lashing the fake boy on the real rubber mattress and a whole group was painting squares of Styrofoam blue. These were to keep the children on station in the water, but they didn't really work.

The children were delivered to White Foot where they ate the ship out of doughnuts and bagels before descending like locusts on the City of Chappaquiddick and the electric barge. Roy Campbell didn't want them on board his tug - he had been that route before.

Joe was exasperated by the delays but finally the fake boy was positioned, the children were positioned, the camera rolled and the shark came up nowhere near the mattress. So, the boat took the children out of the water, another boat rearranged the boy on the mattress, the shark was realigned and then the children were put back in the water. But now they drifted with the change of current. This time when the cameras rolled, the shark rose too far out of the water, so the boat came for the children, a boat went to position the mattress, and so it continued until the sun moved from its position and nothing could be done about that.

"Now I see why it's taken them all summer," said a saddened and wiser Joe, as he went off to try his luck with other scenes.

It was not until afternoon that the summer's work came to its gory end before a battery of cameras lined up behind the battlements on Garage Sale's roof. Every camera with every type of lens was there, so there was going to be enough footage to satisfy even perfectionist Steve.

But would the shark's head explode? It had been filled with 10 gallons of "blood and guts" and four sticks of dynamite. However, it'd set out there in the salt damp all night and there was consternation that they were not going to get the bang out of it they'd planned.

Just in case, some of the less brave removed themselves to White Foot, while others got out of range on the smaller boats. They needn't have bothered - up went the head, looking more like a pink variation of Old Faithful than a blowing up shark and it was all over.

Gulls came in to look over the edible debris while Special Effects picked up the rest.

Verna Fields came out and she and Joe set up the final sinking of the Orca. When she sank beneath the service for the last time, and as the final bubble had surfaced, there was a great cheer which resounded throughout Edgartown Harbor. The movie was over, finished, and they can go home.

Early the next morning Barbara Bass and Verna Fields anti-climatically snuck over to Vineyard Haven with a small camera crew and filmed the closing of the doors of the ferry "Islander" behind a horde of people and gear (some of it belonging to *Jaws*) bound off-Island. It was the final shot, and "symbolic" thought Barbara.

AS THE LAST SHOUT ECHOED IN THE HARBOR, OUTSIZED BRAND-NEW TRUCKS ARRIVED AND, BEFORE THE WEEK WAS OUT, JAWS WAS GONE.

THE ISLAND HAD NOT CHANGED BUT SOME OF THE PEOPLE HAD. SEVERAL WOMEN FOLLOWED MEN THEY HAD MET TO CALIFORNIA, AND SOME GOT MARRIED. A LITTLE BOY HAD A NEW BIKE AND A CARPENTER HAD A NEW TRUCK. THE KELLEY HOUSE AND THE BOATYARD WERE OUT OF DEBT AND MRS. CARROLL GOT A TRIP TO GREECE. BARBARA NEVIN WENT HOME TO CLEAN HOUSE AND JONATHAN FILLEY WAS IN ANOTHER MOVIE IN HOLLYWOOD. THE GIRL PHOTOGRAPHER WAS SMELLING BETTER AND EVERYONE WAS HOPING THE MOVIE WOULD BE A SUCCESS SO THEY COULD WATCH IT FOR YEARS ON THE LATE SHOW.

NOT A SIGN WAS LEFT (EXCEPT, PERHAPS, IN BANK ACCOUNTS) THAT AN EFFORT SIMILAR TO A SMALL WAR HAD BEEN WAGED ON MARTHA'S VINEYARD.

45 YEARS LATER

Hello again fellow Finatics. Michael here, and I hope you enjoyed going on the amazing adventure that Edith Blake provided you. This book, and Carl Gottlieb's "The *Jaws* Log," published a month later, provided an amazing look behind the scenes of the making of a film that, 45 years later, is still regarded as a classic. A lot has happened, both on Martha's Vineyard and off, since *Jaws* premiered on June 20, 1975, and I thought it important to end this project with an update.

The Island of Martha's Vineyard is pretty much as pristine today as it was in 1974. There still is no McDonald's on the Island. They tried to put one on the Island in 1979 and the proposal was quickly voted down by the residents. Soon afterwards, the six towns that comprise Martha's Vineyard passed an ordinance to keep Mickey D's and all other similar enterprises from building on the Island. In fact, the only "chain" businesses are two Stop and Shop stores (formerly part of the A&P chain) and a Dairy Queen that Dick Brown built on the Island in 1967. And while this may be unfortunate news for unaware visitors craving a Big Mac, it's amazing news for *Jaws* fans as the Island looks almost exactly as it did when the film was made.

Take a walk-through Edgartown and you'll recognize the famous crosswalk where Brody tells Hendricks to "let Polly do the printing." Go inside the Edgartown Town Hall and you're immediately sent back into the selectmen's room where Quint announced his presence by dragging his fingernails down the chalkboard. In the past I have likened a trip to Martha's Vineyard by *Jaws* fans with fans of "Star Trek" getting to visit the U.S.S Enterprise. Many fans, myself included, have learned where the various filming locations are (a group of fans, including Jim Beller and John Campopiano, have created "The Ultimate Location Guide," which can be found online) but even the newcomer to the Island will easily recognize the dock where the tiger shark hung as well as the two ferries (On Time II and On Time III) which will take you over to Chappaquiddick Island, where the final resting place of Pipit the dog is located.

Martha's Vineyard is still the place to go for the politically famous. Woodrow Wilson Sayre lived on the Island until his death in September 2002, though he is buried in Washington D.C. Bill Clinton has visited the Island many times and John Kennedy, Jr. was heading to Martha's Vineyard when he had his tragic plane accident. Most recently, in August 2019, Barack Obama purchased a home on the Island.

Sadly, many of the Islanders mentioned in the book who had a large part in the making of the film have passed on, including Dr. Robert Nevin and his wife, Barbara, Bob Carroll, Lynn Murphy, Herschel West, Craig Kingsbury, and Chris Rebello, who sadly passed away at the age of 37 after suffering a heart attack. Even sadder, as I was literally finishing this chapter, word came that Lee Fierro, who played Mrs. Kintner in the film and was loved worldwide by *Jaws* fans, had passed away. Those still with us include Jonathan Filley, who is now a successful film producer; Jeffrey Kramer, also a producer who became, along with his co-producers, the first to win television's Emmy Award for both the year's Outstanding Drama Series AND Outstanding Comedy Series in the same year, which he achieved in 1999. Jeffrey Voorhees escaped off his raft and has been the manager of the Wharf Pub for almost 30 years. Michael Haydn, the guitar player on the beach at the beginning of the film, studied at Boston's Berklee College of Music and still performs on Martha's Vineyard. Today, long-time Island resident Donna Honig is the go-to person when fans of the film visit Martha's Vineyard. If Finatics were inspired by royalty, she would certainly be the Queen of Amity.

Of course, *Jaws* has cast its shadow far beyond the Vineyard. In Hollywood, it set many records, including becoming the first film to gross $100 million domestically. In a world where some of today's new films make that amount and more in a single weekend, it is an achievement to be lauded. In fact, when adjusted for inflation, *Jaws* is the 7th most popular film in history. It also introduced us to the "summer blockbuster," a period capitalized on now when popular action films are released to take advantage of schools being out. It made stars out of its three lead actors (Robert Shaw sadly passed away much too soon in 1978; Roy Scheider died three decades later) and helped introduce one of the most popular and critically acclaimed filmmakers in the history of Hollywood to the world in Steven Spielberg. *Jaws* won three Academy Awards (for Sound, Verna Fields' editing and John Williams' iconic musical score) and pretty much introduced a new genre' to the industry. Shark-themed films, from *Deep Blue Sea* (1999) to *Open Water* (2003), from *The Shallows* (2016) to *The MEG* (2018) have come and gone, but none of them have come near the originality, or the terror, of *Jaws*.

And, on a more personal note, *Jaws* has created an amazing legion of fans. Some, like me, have been fans of the film since 1975. And, like myself, fans such as Jim Beller, Eddie McCormack, Dana Goudreault, Matt Drinnenberg, Peter Spadetti, Eric Augustin, Mark Fitzgibbons, Jamie Saunders, Jay Shinn, and many others have amassed amazing memorabilia collections, ranging from movie posters to the actual fighting chair (and fishing rod) Quint used in the film. Some fans turned their passion for the film into art. Jake Gove, James Gelet, Erik Hollander and Michael Roddy spent years putting together the ultimate fan documentary film, *The Shark is Still Working* (2007). Michael Schultz used his artistic talents to start Shark City Ozark, where fans can purchase hand sculpted versions of Bruce the Shark in various sizes. You can find them on Facebook. Film director Kevin Smith was so inspired by the film that several of his movies include homages to it while "The Walking Dead" make up master and director Greg Nicotero not only created a life-size replica of the shark's head for the first JawsFEST in 2005 but also a life-size display of the three stars standing at the back of the ORCA for the 2012 *Jaws*FEST. Nicotero also oversaw the restoration of "Junkyard Bruce," the last remaining shark made from the original mold that for over 30 years sat in a tree in a Los Angeles-area junkyard and will soon be the centerpiece for the newly constructed Academy Museum of Motion Pictures.

Finally, on an even more personal note, *Jaws* has been an amazing influence on ME. I met my best friend of four-plus decades because of the film. And I've made hundreds of friends the world over because of our shared love of *Jaws*. Hell, I wouldn't be here writing this if the film hadn't had such a profound effect on me. I've made many pilgrimages to Martha's Vineyard and have even shared the log cabin that Steven Spielberg and others lived in during production with some fellow fans. Sadly, the cabin was torn down on September 8, 2006, but a piece of it sits on my desk to this day, reminding me of fun times spent with friends.

I'll close by speaking for all the Finatics and say "thank you" to the cast and crew of *Jaws*. You gave the world a true film classic and you gave my friends and I something we can share with each other. And a very special "thank you" to Edith Blake. If she hadn't answered her telephone so many years ago, you may never have read this.

BONUS PHOTO SECTION

TO HELP CELEBRATE THE 45TH ANNIVERSARY OF JAWS WE HAVE SELECTED A COLLECTION OF PHOTOS TAKEN BY EDITH BLAKE IN 1974, MANY OF THEM NEVER BEFORE SEEN AND INCLUDED HERE FOR THE FIRST TIME.

This is one of the photos Edith Blake sent Michael Smith in 1976. He had both Richard Dreyfuss and Roy Scheider sign it. Both actors were delighted with the photo.

Brody (Roy Scheider) and Cassidy (Jonathan Filley) walk the "deserted" beach.

Deputy Hendricks (Jeffrey Kramer) Brody and Cassidy find the crab covered remains of Chrissie Watkins.

Setting up the Alex Kintner attack.

Spending some time in the sun.

Quint (Robert Shaw) and his mate (Hershel West) stroll through the streets of Amity.

The town waits the Council's decision.

Taking things under advisement (l-r) Cyprian Dube, Murray Hamilton, Bob Carroll, Philip Norton, Alfred Wilde)

Scheider takes a smoke break between shots.

Quints drawing.

Taking a break.

The Amity Music Store

Steven Spielberg directs Paul Goulart and Dorothy Fielding in a deleted scene.

Spielberg and co-star/co-writer Carl Gottlieb take in the tiger shark.

The motley crew of fishermen with their catch.

"Stick your head in there and find out if it's a man eater!"

Hooper (Richard Dreyfuss) measures the bite radius.

Another photo Edith Blake sent Michael.
On the back she wrote, "He is yelling JAWS!"

Dreyfuss cooling off during the Beach Panic scene.

Spielberg and Dreyfuss confer in the Atlantic.

Cooling off on the set.

Selectman in the surf

The estuary victim (Ted Grossman) having a bad day.

Stuffing the sharks head for the explosive finale'

Brody heading up to the crow's nest.

"Smile"

Roll end credits.

Scheider awaits hit turn at bat.

Dreyfuss holds Scheider on first.

Keeping his eye on the ball.

Coffee....breakfast of Champions!

Installing letters on the ORCA

Quints fighting chair.

The ORCA ready to set sail.

The ORCA in all her night time glory.

The legendary Bob Mattey.

Anybody home?

You missed a spot.

Preparing the "Island" theatre for the Island Premiere.

Vineyard's glamorous people attend the Island premiere.

EXPANDED 50TH ANNIVERSARY EDITION

HELLO, AGAIN

I can't believe it's been five years since I had the honor of updating Edie's book. I also can't believe I have the honor of doing it again as both this book and the film celebrate their 50lth Anniversary this year. Where has the time gone?

In that time, not surprisingly, the popularity of *Jaws* has continued to grow. New books, magazines, games, action figures and honest-to-goodness live theater productions have inspired another generation of fans. Many of the remaining cast and crew members, including Richard Dreyfuss, Jeffrey Kramer, Jeff Voorhees, Carl Gottlieb Joe Alves and Ted Grossman continue to draw legions of fans when they appear at celebrity shows. And, fingers crossed, by the time you are reading this, a third Official *Jaws* Celebration will have been announced.

The Vineyard is still a "go to" place for politicians. Shortly before this book was reissued in 2020, the 44th President of the United States, Barack Obama, and his wife Michelle, moved to the Island. An Island resident told me that once the Obamas called the Island their home the Internet on the Island worked much better! In an amazing case of life imitating art, Jonathan Searle, the young boy who, along with his brother Steven, panicked swimmers in the waters of Amity by swimming by with a fake shark fin on their back, was named Police Chief of Oak Bluffs, one of the towns on Martha's Vineyard. Jonathan Filley continues to work in Hollywood, producing such popular television programs as "Elementary," "The Blacklist," and "Succession," for which he received an Emmy Award nomination for Outstanding Drama Series. Jeff Voorhees retired from the Wharf and now splits his time between the Vineyard and Florida. Jeffrey Kramer continues to work and oversee his production company, Juniper Place Productions. On a more personal note, Jeff has become a great friend whose kindness and continued support are greatly appreciated. Michael Haydn continues to perform on the Island while Donna Honig conducts location tours for fans.

Sadly, not all the *Jaws*-related news these past five years has been good. On November 8, 2023, artist Roger Kastel, who created the iconic art used for both the paperback edition of Peter Benchley's novel as well as the film's poster, passed away. Oddly enough, I had been chatting with Susan Backlinie about Mr. Kastel the weekend before he passed when I spoke with her at an event in Lexington, Kentucky. Six months later, on May 11, 2024, Susan left us. Most recently, Susan Murphy who, along with her husband, Captain Lynn Murphy, was instrumental in the making of the film, passed away on August 6, 2024. I had the amazing opportunity of visiting them at their home and boatyard in 2006. I not only got to stand next to Hooper's boat, the Fascinatin' Rhythm, as well as hold the actual controls for the shark, but Captain Murphy gave me an actual piece of the ORCA II.

But the hardest passing for me came on February 25, 2023. That is the day we lost Edith Blake.

EDIE

I can honestly say that I never met a woman like Edith Blake. Fiercely independent, she didn't suffer fools easily. She was 97 when she passed, which in itself is an amazing feat. Even more amazing, she continued to play tennis competitively well into her 90s. If they ever made a film about her – and, over the years, there have been inquiries by various agencies interested in doing just that - and you could have one actress from history portray her, your only choice would be Katharine Hepburn.

Born in New Jersey on September 13, 1925, Edith was the daughter of Philip Sands Graham and Eleanor Belmont Degener. Her paternal grandparents, Robert Graham and Edith Sands, were both summer visitors to the Martha's Vineyard town of Edgartown, Massachusetts. Edith first visited the Island in 1936 and was a constant visitor until she moved there permanently in the mid-1960s. She was hired by Henry Beetle Hough, the editor of the Vinyard "Gazette" newspaper, as a full-time writer and photographer. The two married in 1979 and remained together until Mr. Hough's death in 1985.

She left the newspaper in 1969, striking out on her own as a freelance reporter. While she still contributed stories and photos to the "Gazette," her work also appeared in several magazines, including *Sail, On the Sound, Yank* and *Nature*. She published two books: 1969's "Doorways, Lanterns and Fences of Martha's Vineyard – A Photographic Essay" and, of course, the book you're currently reading, which she self-published. My thanks to Bow Van Riper from the Martha's Vineyard Museum for providing some of the above biographical information.

Long time friend, and Island resident, Donna Honig first met Edith when Donna's father, a photographer for the Associated

Press, was sent to the Island to cover the inquest into the actions of Senator Edward Kennedy, who on July 18, 1969, had driven off a bridge on Chappaquiddick Island, killing his passenger, Mary Jo Kopechne. Donna worked at a local beauty salon and did Edie's mother's hair. She began doing Edie's hair in 1980. When Donna left to open her own salon, Edie went with her. Donna continued to do her hair until her death. Donna remembers that Edie rarely cooked, only going to the supermarket once in a blue moon. She preferred to share her meals with friends in Edgartown. She also loved her fans. According to Donna, Edie never really understood the impact her book has had with fans from all over the world and would chat with them often, usually while doing book signings on the porch of Edgartown Books. I had the great honor of joining her for a book signing in September 2021. Not only would she chat with the fans, but she insisted in writing a little passage before signing her name. Her independence was on full display when I went to meet her car. I offered my hand to help her out and she just ignored it, getting out on her own, though she did allow me the honor of escorting her up the stairs, her hand holding firmly on to my arm.

Later that night she joined myself, my wife and a group of fans for dinner at the Wharf, where she held court for all in attendance. We were also joined for dinner by Michael Haydn, who also shared some amazing stories of Vineyard life, including the fact that he had to go to the rear of the local music store in order to purchase Elvis Presley albums! Dinner also featured an appearance by Jeff Voorhees, who posed for photos with all who asked him. After dinner, I walked her to her car and we said our goodbyes. That was the last time I saw her. However, her stories, her memories, and her incredible kindness to a 16-year-old boy so long ago will never be forgotten.

Like many fans, I will be visiting the Island this summer for the 50lth Anniversary of *Jaws*. And while I will enjoy spending time with friends and fans from all over the world, I will also feel a touch of sadness because Edie won't be there. However, I know her spirit will be and that gives me great comfort.

Michael A. Smith
March 2025

Edith Blake presiding over a book signing at Edgartown Books.

ONE MORE LOOK

Shortly after the 45th Anniversary edition of this book was released in 2020, Edith Blake came across a set of additional negatives from her time on the set of *Jaws* and donated them to the Martha's Vineyard Museum. After some intense research (thank you, Eric Augustin), to my knowledge the majority of these new images have never been published before now. With my genuine thanks again to Bow Van Riper from the Martha's Vineyard Museum, I present them to you here.

PHOTOS

Joe Alves on the Orca.

The tow fin.

Giving Teddy Grossman a closer look.

Packing the shark head for the final scene.

Testing, testing.

Getting some foreground on the pulpit.

The Orca in Menemsha.

The Orca II

The Orca II going under.

Fritzi Jane Courtney and Lorraine Gary work om their tans.

"Jaws" author Peter Benchley reports the news.

Fourth of July beach

Who's got the football?

Nervous onlookers.

Cyprien R. Dube getting set for the showdown with Brody at the Town Hall.

Roy Scheider and Jeffrey Kramer discuss Mrs. Kintner's bounty offer.

It wasn't me!

On Location.... On Martha's Vineyard • 185

Getting into position.

Waiting for the call of "action"

Taking aim.

BOOM!

Heading home.

The film premier on the Island.

ABOUT THE AUTHOR

Edith Blake, who hails from Bernardsville, New Jersey, is more closely associated with Martha's Vineyard where she represented the fourth generation of confirmed Edgartown adherents. She has been a ranked tennis player, raced in the crew of large yawls and, after many intermediate berths, became Captain of her own 11-footer.

She contributed to *Yankee, Sail, On* the *Sound, Nature* magazine and others while her writings and photographs appeared for many years in the Vineyard *Gazette*. She was an authoritative author in the field of architecture and had a great passion for bird photography.

Edith Blake passed away on February 25, 2023 on Martha's Vineyard. She was 97.

Edith Blake and her dog outside the "Spielberg Cabin"
(photo credit – Dana L. Goudreault)

Printed in Dunstable, United Kingdom